and sketches of their intimate

Other entries reflect the inception & growth process of ideas later to be fully realized in book form (<u>Cities</u>; <u>Freeways</u>; <u>New York New York</u>; <u>The RSVP Cycles</u>) or in built form (The Portland fountains). Still others relate the Halprins' recent involvement with community workshops, group sessions, & participatory planning. In short, the full range of Halprin's imagination & professional activity is displayed.

The material here represents about 1/12 of the original notebooks, and was selected by an associate, Jim Burns, on the grounds that someone close to Halprin's work, but at one remove from his total personal involvement, could best present a cross section equally accenting past interests & current concerns. The notebooks are entirely written in Halprin's own hand, which is rather more legible than this one.

—Randall Goff—The MIT Press—   Jan '72

. . . .

The MIT Press has also published Halprin's <u>Cities</u> in a revised paperback edition. This edition contains new material on the fountains designed by Halprin.

10⁰⁰

LAWRENCE HALPRIN

notebooks 1959 1971

The MIT Press
Cambridge, Massachusetts, and
London, England.

contents

Introduction

These notebooks started, if I recall correctly, about 12 years ago..... the occasion causing them was Peter Shepheard's trip from England to visit me in Marin County .... He came, he said when he introduced himself, to see my gardens and to try to understand how I worked ---- in retrospect it was our mutual interest then in ecology as a determinant of form & process which made us so quickly warm to each other — at a time when formalistic contrivances & personal 2-dimensional calligraphy dominated much of the design & attitude toward gardens ....

I remember travelling up onto the high meadows on the haunches of Mt. Tamalpais & discussing the way grass-lands grew on the serpentine .... how the redwood groves climbed up in the crevices between the mountain folds and hung in the shaded, moister high valleys -- while the oak & the madrone & the buckeye found their homes on the sunlit & baked exposed flanks ------ we talked, I recall, of how these natural configurations caused form & how logical & understandable that was --- as against contrivances & patterns on the ground • no matter how pretty ------ we also talked biology & plants & birds & animals & Peter carried along with him a notebook, in which, from time to time, he made beautiful sketches or notes ------ I was really delighted with it!!

My own note-taking had always been very sporadic ---- usually on bits of paper - or whatever sketchbook came to hand ----- mostly in the form of drawings ------ Many of these are now lost, or misplaced, or scattered in various parts of the world ....

I am grateful, however, that most of the sketches that I made during the war years are NOT lost ..... they are not simply because of a "fluke" !!

My destroyer was steaming towards the invasion of OKINAWA --- while underway I put all the sketches I had been making, together in a packet — along with some letters — & threw them across to another ship which, for reasons I do not now remember, was steaming back to the States ..... "AT least Ann will see what I've been up to, I thought".

Several days later during the invasion, while on 'Radar picket duty', we were hit (right where my bunk was) in the forward section of our ship, by a kamikaze plane ----- the drawings were safe-

-- the ship, the USS MORRIS DD 417- & many of her crew were not ----

4

Jap body floating Sim
Fake Bay Oct. 22.   Halpin

Lake Sentani
Oct 9
Hollandia

6

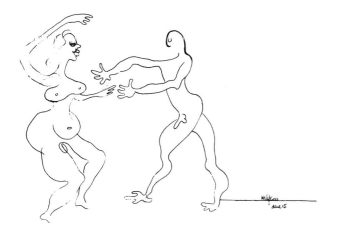

At all events — inspired by the consistency of Peter's note-taking, I started my own special notebooks & have continued them ever since .... The entries have, of course, ebbed & flowed — more consistently in some periods than others. At the beginning most of the books are filled with special events like trips, or strong impressions .... More recently they have taken the form of a professional diary or travelling office if you will. Since I am more & more away from home & office, the notebook (always at hand) makes it easier to record impressions & note down ideas at any & all times ... it lets thought processes flow & find expression.

People "think" in different ways, & I find that I think most effectively graphically & also that my thinking is influenced a great deal by my ability to get it down where I can "look at it" & think about it further ---- the process of thinking with me generates more thinking ---- the notebooks, in other

words have not only been a way of
"recording" ideas but also of "generating"
ideas ---- they are ways of running
out what I call series of alternative SCORES.

I have had several rules for myself
in the notebooks: one of which is never to
cut out pages & throw them away.... that,
in retrospect, has been a good idea —
many thoughts or sketches which I hated at
the time, in the passage of years, generated
others which now seem to have validity ---
I also have not added to or subtracted
from the notebooks ..... they remain as
they come ....

NOT all my ideas are in notebooks -
(naturally), nor necessarily are all my first
idea sketches of projects .... some of these
still find their way to scraps of paper or
tracing paper & are in the office files ......
BUT this is a book on notebooks & has
been kept literally to that .... we have not
attempted (except for the war sketches) to
include any material not directly drawn
or written in my notebooks...........

Some themes crop up over & over again & I expect will continue to do so --- nature walks & hikes & a constant reference to natural phenomena & processes recur consistently —— they are root sources for me! For that reason MT. Tamalpais, Phoenix Lake, & Camp Tucker sketches are legion here .... these are trails & walks in a magnificent STATE Park & Water District region in Marin County where I live which continually inspires me & to which I constantly return for spiritual & ecological sustenance ·······

Two other Nature resources have formed me & the NOTEBOOKS ---- the great 'range of light' called Sierra Nevada where for many summers I have immersed myself in mountain ranges & water courses & their processes · & the North Coast of California where we have a cabin & where the interface between land & Sea with its tremendous surf, its rocks & sea birds, whales & seals & the romantic abalone engulf me in movement & natural choreographies.

Movement & choreography have always been a consistent influence on me & my work... natural movements characterized by water & natural forces & the evidence of natural change over time have led me to my endless fascination with natural processes ———

Man-made movement, particularly in theatre & dance, through joint work with my wife, the dancer Ann Halprin, brought me to investigations into ways of designating & designing for movement -- these I called MOTATION ...... Later these led to explorations into Processes-over-time & the notion of SCORING & the understanding of its KEY role in the way we arrive at solutions .....

For these reasons I became involved in a series of experimental workshops called "Experiments in Environment". These workshops are ways of exploring the interrelationships between man & his environment & of the influence of people working together on what emerges from these explorations .. Workshops have been increasingly important for me in exploring with groups of colleagues & students the root sources of "environments" through experience <u>not</u> discussion alone ---- we have now begun to develop the workshop techniques into tools by which citizens in their own communities make significant input into planning their own environments.

That is what the P⊕S cycles (R / V) (which forms the basis of my philosophy of working) -- is about --- both as a book & as a way of looking at the world & working within it . . . .

P⊕S (R / V) originated from the workshops & then was developed in the notebooks . . . . it is a way of making things visible & of describing & working <u>with</u> process towards <u>objectives</u> rather than toward predetermined <u>goals</u> . . . . it is open & inclusive rather than closed & exclusive – a way of making multiple input possible & of encouraging groups of people – through

the cycles to influence & be accountable
for their own destiny in art & life ......

These notebooks have, in the same
way been - for me - a process .... a
way of exploring ideas & of 'scoring' the
future .... they are filled with the trying-
out of things ..... of alternative scores <u>S</u>
which have then been either discarded or
re-cycled into actuality or put aside for
other times .... they are full of letters either
sent or not sent, articles published or never
submitted for publication, speeches made or
only imagined ----- an assemblage.

Making the selection of what should
be included in this book from the more
than 4-5000 pages in the notebooks was, in
itself, a difficult task... I felt strongly that
I could not make the selections myself -
that would have been like evaluating your
own fantasies --- so I turned to my good
friend & colleague <u>JIM BURNS</u>
who agreed to take on the task for me...
I am delighted with what he has done
& wish here to gratefully express my

deep appreciation to him .. I sense that he was guided by a clear understanding of the basic forces which underlie my work & also that he attempted, through the selections to emphasize the growth & change in my professional life rather than the purely personal & family events in the notes.

In the early notebooks there is emphasis on gardens & on landscape .... the later notebooks reflect my increasing interest & commitment to the total environment as an integrating matrix for "community" :— that is its existence for us NOT apart but we as part & parcel of it ... the basic notion of ECOSYSTEM ----

For that reason I have become more & more involved with city & urban problems since it is here that so many of the most searing & demanding of our environmental — social problems are concentrated ..... I am committed to the idea that there is an inevitable feed-back between an environment & its inhabitants --- that one affects the other

& in that sense ecological & social principles are the same. For that reason I have worked at planning large urban regions but also, with equal interest & intensity, have designed plazas & streets at the micro-urban scale ....

For me, the idea of garden includes the total environment of man ... the whole world viewed as an ecological unit where man & nature together must, I believe, form community or else we will not survive .... I have always felt that-- it is simply that, in recent years I have had more opportunity to express it & work with it .....

Personally my own development has broadened to a deeper understanding of process ..... as a biological force generating form, but perhaps more importantly as group interaction dynamically thrusting toward valid human solutions .....

Finally, I would like to thank all the good friends (and all my foes)

who appear in the notes & the
drawings ---- all of whom helped in
the generative interaction & often clash
of ideas (even some irreconcilable ones)
from which, of course, energy flows &
things happen ...... I would like
also to thank the many friends &
colleagues over the years in my office
& in workshops - out of dialogues with
whom many of these ideas emerged.. my
family which fills this notebook in
so many visible & invisible ways -
ANN - DARIA - RANA & then the multi-
faceted, difficult, intricate & incredibly
beautiful world through which we move
& have our being ....

Lawrence Halprin
San Francisco
September 1971.....

16

waterfall in
Partington creek
Nov 28-59

Annie m Lime kiln
creek MAY 27-1960

18

Father's day hike with Darca who gave me the ——— view down from MT. TAM.
hike as a father's day present.   June 19 - 1960

Room | RENAISSANCE PROGRAM | 79 × 59 — 30 | Rehearsal - @ gym - | June 23, 1960

for U.C. Extension program | platforms. | 4×8' up 24" | Dance.

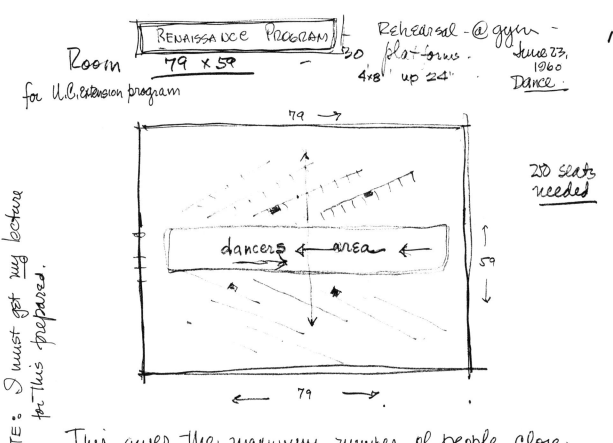

79 →

59

79

250 seats needed

This gives the maximum number of people close to the dancers and also the closest sense of contact between dancers & audience

also: dancers use entire length of the space rather than working against it.

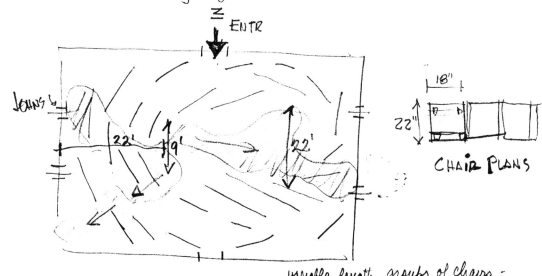

N
ENTR

JOHNS &

22'   9'   22'

18"

22"

CHAIR PLANS

VARIATION -   variable length groups of chairs - broken aisles between — oval - not linear

Evening Rehearsal June 29 for *
Renaissance in S.F. program
@ Extension division gymnasium

figures
warming up.

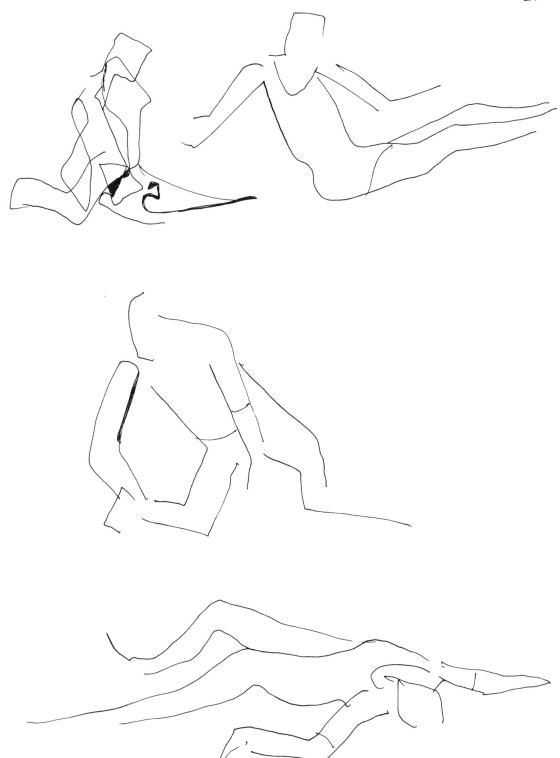

movement starts in circle - all related
then break out & self-contained becoming
non-related.

demonstration - the creative process
movement in space.

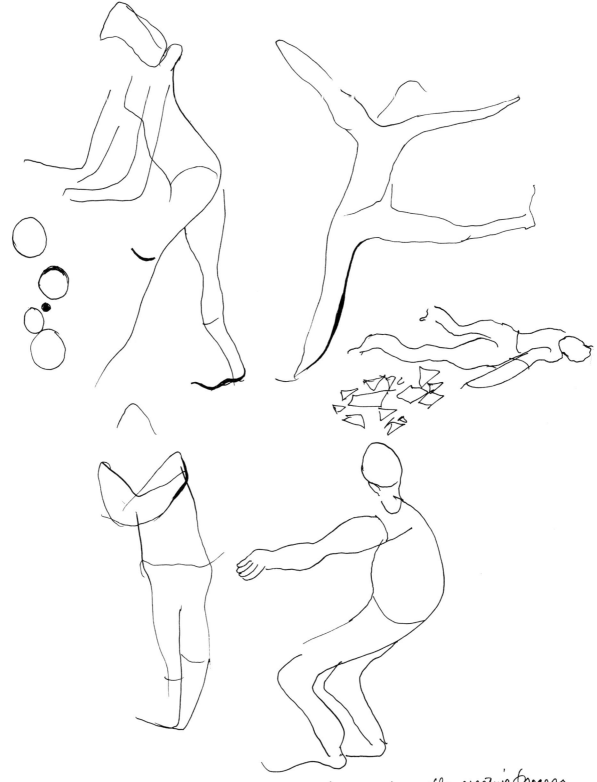

demonstration - the creative process
movements in space - self contained then related to
each other - then to space

HIKE NOTES - JULY 3 - 1960 -

Phoenix Canyon - N from Kent --

Buckeyes @ End of flowering - still some conical candles.
leaves beginning to turn brown.
First in thru' dry hillside facing S.W. with the variegated
greens of rwd, bay, fir &c xcross canyon on N. slope of TAM
HOT. ·· DRY....
Then around bend into moist
canyon & the flowing tinkle
of stream cool in the deep moist
canyon -

Rwds, sword fern, alder, thin bay.
Smell very aromatic on this hot day.

deep woods -

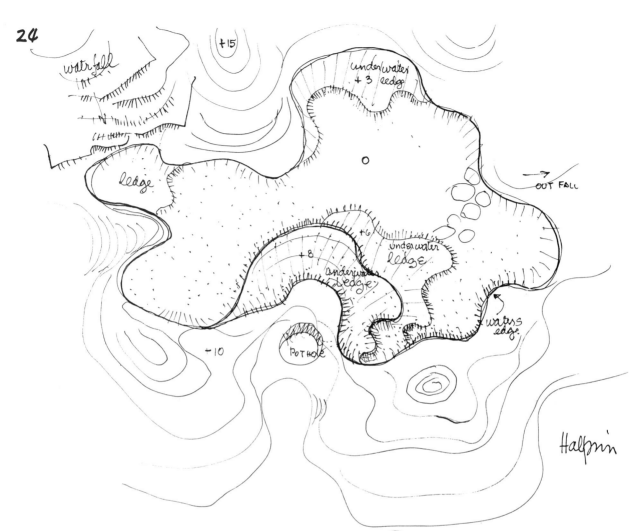

Swimming hole above waterfall in the Tuolumne river.
water falls across ledges into deep pot hole - granite
sloping to bottom all around edges - ledges @ different elevations
underwater make fine places to lie or paddle
with deepest in one place - 50' × 30' overall
swelling granite sides around - to lie on - with some levels.

Hi-Sierra
Aug 6, 1960

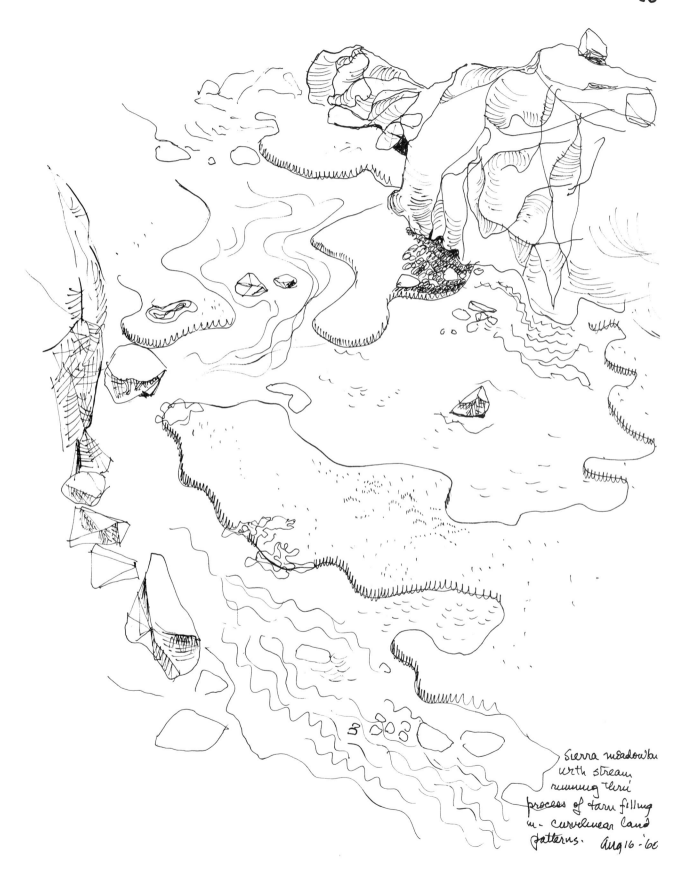

Sierra meadow/ar
with stream
running thru
process of tarn filling
in curvilinear land
patterns.   Aug 16 - '6c

Halprin

Sierra water course 1 water curves
around great granite boulders - then falls over
jumble of intermediate size rocks going over
the flat ones & under & between the round
velocity speeds up as water forced through
small orifices - slow as sheets out below fall

Sierra Watercourse
2.

Halprin

Water sheeting over great
smooth granite blocks & at
bottom banging against a boulder
creating great turbulence.

Sierra watercourse #3

Halprin

Sierra watercourse #5
cascade above midnight lake - small
volume of water trickling over striated granite ledges.

at Punk's cabin—
Sept 4 - 1960
along coast

Everything in motion - water, rocks, sea weed.
air currents, birds great baroque
composition - all echoing each other

GARDENS
OF THE
HIGH
SIERRA

1 - Art by accident uses the
same processes as exist in
natural phenomena — up in
the Sierra see it clearly.

2 - Natural phenomena give us
the base on which we hang
our sense of art organization.

3 - Art as Science is a search
for this existing natural
organization.

The Community in the landscape — a man made landscape

①

ON HILLS

Brisbane
Corte Madera
vertical streets,
Sausalito

Greenbrae +
contoured streets.

ON FLAT,

Belvedere

Terra Linda
Levittown

The street

Easter
Hill
Belvedere

Corte Madera
Larkspur

The Common

Greenwood
Common

Belvedere

Married students housing

use of natural features

S.F. Row
housing

What is new in our communities is SPREAD & number

Before this we have had nodules, concentrated groups. with a
        kind of gem-like quality - hard & tight & facetted

Now we SPREAD into the landscape.

This is OK if there is estate-space between so that roads
        & buildings are separated by either the existing or
        the planted landscape

But now the voids of the tiny estates (60×110) have closed
        down so the roads are bigger than the gardens &
        the houses dwarf the landscape — on into infinity.

And FORMALISTIC maneuvers do not solve this

Plan-like geometries beg the issue & fail

An imposed geometry will fail.

We need to design into the landscape in a naturalistic
        way so that communities merge & become landscape.
        Not copy nature but use her processes to evolve
        patterns of growth so that communities become part
        of a landscape. Nature & natural processes.

Statues & urns in Tuileries garden
The pedestals are far more important &
well designed than the "objets" they support!

Paris has <u>no</u> skyline - It is beautiful at ground
level largely becuz of its open spaces - It also
on the whole lacks beautiful buildings - it is the
vistas & plazas backed up by mass plantings
which create the great effects.

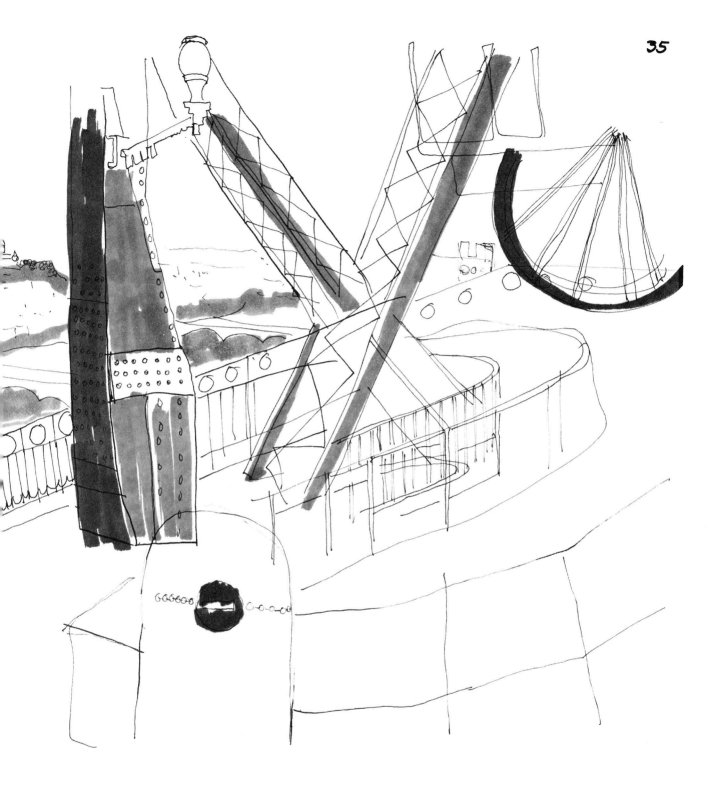

Paris from the restaurant
2ᴱ stage – Eiffel tower

wednesday- July 7ᵗʰ 1961

Israel
June 1961

NOTES AT Ein Hashofet

get PLANT LIFE · (a Scientific American book.)
published by SIMON & SHUSTER
Lib Congr. # 57-7951

Conversions   1.610 kilometer = mile

$$Fahrenheit = \frac{9}{5} C + 32$$

$$Centigrade = \frac{5}{9} (F - 32)$$

This is a complete community combining all facilities: living + agriculture + factories + elementary & High Schools. It also includes social & cultural activities i.e. Library, auditorium 1500 seats, swimming, sports, eating, music hall - movies, concerts etc. It remains however non urban - possibly closer to suburban than anything - more suburban I think than farm-like in our sense. There is little sense of mechanized mobility - a couple of cars & trucks for special use.

The landscape is dominant. When the group first arrived 21 years ago there was nothing but rocks. (see pictures). they immediately planted trees - mostly Pinus halepensis (was there a plan then? this would be interesting) but also carobs, casuarina, Pinus canariensis & Pinea Dahlbergia (from India) jacaranda (doesn't do very well) olives in rows etc. Then buildings By now the buildings are covered by the trees and the new ones are being built in what amounts to a man made forest. (see my photo) The difficult existing environment - great heat in the summers & bad winds in the winter have been very largely overcome by these plantations of trees.

Ein Hashofet continued

This community has been built in a man made
park & forest. And in that sense it is a garden community
In general most trees were planted on ten foot centers
in orchard rows & this doesn't seem any too close.
The soil is very shallow - about. 8" - 10" & is
underlain by solid limestone - see my photo
which percolates water through fissures but
otherwise is impervious. Both the ph & the depths of soil
have controlled the kinds of trees

Everyone agrees that lawn is the best ground cover -
you can walk on it - it cools the atmosphere & with
power mowers its easier to maintain than ground covers
on the whole they tend to stay away from heavily paved
spaces & there is a real interesting emotional attachment
to gardens & gardening. I think it came about by contrast
with the natural environment which is _so_ harsh, And
is in direct contrast with the typical Arab kind of
thing which is no garden in the accepted sense but
all paved (with dirt or stone & architectonic) I wonder
if any kibbutz has tried to solve things in this way?

COST OF COURSE would be a factor
Typical average plan 4 BR unit
No privacy on the whole
is attempted between the
gardens.
So far I have seen little
private outdoor living - community only.

Grass
plains
↑forest

North ←
↑wind

There are also great forests "built" between the communities (pictures from Keren Kayemeth) which continue the sense
of green forest over the hills.

Trees were according to Keren Kayemeth trials which
had been in effect for 9 years - P. halepensis (best) canary
casuarina, brush, P. capresin (cypress not good)
none of the trees give fruit & of small amt soil.
Walnuts are fine

don't take any hired help also don't want to
work outside therefore have to keep everyone busy
all year so the ques: what crops to grow but
it is in principle a complete farm + factory
but they are more interested in farming.
     Children can work in farming
     Specialization sets in in factory, not so much
       in agriculture

permanent work   cooperative in city - kibbutz in agriculture

   members - 300 - 40% in production   not counting
   children - 1½ (12 yrs) → 3 hrs @ 18 yr   carpenter
   temporary - ULPAN
       group before OLIM -

Most children stay - could say all

   Tnuvah markets everything -

Part of problem that people come without investment!
Envisions 1000 people

AHUD - 2/3 of ground should be grass.
     entrance on E & " on west side   rains come in
     why continue the boxes to outside ?
     Kidurye - & once every 2 whs for 3 hrs =
       550 cu m /dunam /yr.

according to Yehoshuah Dayan the first trees were planted according to inferences learned by 10 years of Keren Kayemeth trial & error. He feels that the P. halepensis plantings were without any question the most successful.

The ameliorating effect of the forest plantings is very clear. Right now I am sitting on the S.west edge of the Kibbutz (writing) at the end of the plantings. the wind is literally howling in the tops of the trees and is blowing enough to be unpleasant for any length of time. At the same moment inside the Kibbutz by 100' there is hardly any breeze at all.

I find the effect of living in this park-like atmosphere somewhat soporific. It's just like being on a Sierra Club base camp with the tents replaced by permanent houses & the chow line in a [חדר אוכל]. I have a basic criticism to the scheme & that is that everything is too scattered & the spaces are too even throughout. I would like the center to be much denser - exciting all paved with <u>URBAN</u> color & activity & then the houses in this suburban euphoria. Also there should I think be more of a spinal quality to the scheme - a broader central walk - a way to the center & the center stronger.

On plantings: I would like to see the trees grouped more rather than quite so scattered & of course for my taste there is far too much scattered & messy gardening. Lawn! Also as you walk about there ought to be places of interest - statues. rocks - places.

The lack of cars is <u>wonderful</u> - one just went by with visitors on Shabath & it was a real shocker.

I would want more privacy in the gardens by fences or hedges - witness that I feel the end room most desirable so you can get around a corner. also I would like the houses grouped more.

But the gardens make the whole thing possible

This trip brought up the whole question of whether
Israel can afford to preserve wilderness areas.... I believe
that she can and that this ought to be one of them — therefore
preserved intact as a nature preserve — not bastardized by
cleaning up and putting railings around — not
making a swimming pool area out of it — softening the
mystery out of it.

This cityscape is very handsome — the plastic quality of buildings piled up on the hillside approximates as closely as I know the qualities of Aral villages — with no outstanding buildings. (Color could be better). But now Haifa is beginning to lose this with the enormous 12 story scale of flats ON the hills Tops.

view of Haifa from Ron cafe on the Hadar Hacarmel while waiting for Zvi Miller — Sunday June 25 — 1961

EIN OVDAT July 20th
with Yan Jansi + Feipe Yahalom
+ Dan Tsur, Max Jani.

CONVERSATION with George HIM | at Jean Davids house in Tel Aviv Mon nite | June 1961 · 20th

43

graphic artist & designer who designs brochures etc. for EL AL & worlds Fair Israel for Yan.

Question: am I a landscape architect who builds everything architecturally (as Noguchi) ~~&&~~ and "artificially" or tries to make everything look natural.

The fact is of course I do both. But the point is different. The point is, I believe, less and less ~~the~~ form in design as an envelope which is placed around things. What I want is to design events which occur -- which have no necessary or recognizable form but which generate qualities of experience. Thats why I am fascinated by (as who isn't) old streets - colorful people crowding them - non-aligned architecture and a sense of growth. Against that I am bored stiff with architecture which has "form" no matter how beautiful because form is evanescent and intellectual and transient whereas experience in depth of perception is constant.

This is a picturesque, colorful, charming street. It is also dirty, smelly unclean & hopelessly inadequate. But how can we keep the first things which are so wonderful - the fine human scale, the intimate quality the disorder & chance arrangements, the surprises & yet overcome the bad qualities - in modern terms

THIS IS THE MAIN PROBLEM OF MODERN HOUSING.

I am not sure the density is bad!

Since this was built in ancient times there was no access needed for automobiles & the streets are narrow & curling.

Since these people are poor no changes need to be made now to make autos available since they don't have any.

Nothing lines up.

The balconies are askew & at slightly different levels, the roof lines differ - each balcony rail is different & at different heights.

But there is a common bond of materials - stone & some stucco & iron.

On a Shabath walk with Daria along
Rechov. Mamillah - past grandpa Sam's old
office - along the border & no mans land
where we saw some Arab Legionnaires.

Side street off Rechov David.
Hamelech - Sat. morning
June 10th.
1961

Darias questions on the KIBBUTZ
To Yonai Yanai - July 2, 1961

1* Why don't women care about way they look -
e: no lipstick, no high heels.

Y- within our accepted standard they do care.
Don't try to play up to men - not a doll - equality
Also they want to be simple -- farm women.
Dress should be according to individual taste not mass attitude

2* Why do children hate jazz & consider it bad!
But also are very interested in it.

Y- We would like them to appreciate more
serious quiet music
not of lasting value - passing.
we don't particularly try to indoctrinate them
on this but they do know that parents
don't like it.

Daria - says that its just like a folk dance
for us. therefore it can't be wrong.

Y- But its an expression of the going no where
attitude, sexy, provocative. world generation
sexy, drinken.

D- Then you should bring in movies that show
good jazz.

3- D-Why do they think the Arab workers
here are bad ..

Yonai is shocked at this who claims it doesn't
exist. Doesn't believe Daria.

Daria- It might improve the feeling if they
were in better living conditions

Y - can't improve their housing - we don't have enough decent housing for ourselves - our good housing comes by seniority only.

Doesn't think its becuz they are Arabs - anything strange.

D - But children <u>are</u> afraid of them becuz Arabs snicker at them & tease behind them.

Y - Itz becuz Arabs are not accustomed to freedom between the sexes - in Arab villages where have <u>never</u> had any friendships with girls & so react strangely where there <u>is</u> freedom.

4 - Why do <u>all</u> children suck their thumbs.

Y - Our % is not any higher - its just that we see more children together

Not agreed that this is bad for teeth!

Starting to give them pacifiers.

Mebbe there <u>are</u> problems.

NOTE : we have to find concrete differences to express our ideals & ways of living - includes jazz lipstick etc......... Have to set a line of demarcation if give in anywhere whole system breaks down.

5 - Why difference in way handle animals - handle them roughly. Let chickens die. Let puppies die.

Y - Children are farm children - see more of sickness & dying and butchering of chickens - more used to it.

On other hand children are affectionate to own dogs.

48

Danas questions cont'n

Our vet has more important things to do
than dogs

6 - I notice you emphasize arts & crafts
handiworks etc. much more than arithmetic
etc.

Y - Care less about facts & figures than
self expression - but in higher grades do
get back to basics - very high actual criteria.
"LIVING IN SCHOOL" - many social obligations
basically different method - emphasize talks
understanding.

7 - Why do they get up so early - don't.
get enuf' sleep.
But rest in afternoon
So much noise that ~~that~~ get sleep.
End of year

8 - Girls are starting to want to be separated
Ornah says that they are like sisters ~~of~~ and
brothers & it's ok.
Y - mebbe this is is particularly ~~bad~~ worst period
becuz they are just maturing

Ornah - would have usual attitude towards
boys from other groups - their own group
is like brothers - usually don't marry
within group.

There have been discussions on this - when should they change -
Have come to conclusion - this is best system

9- Money does any one get paid ?
No !
allowed a certain amt of expenditures ~~than~~ a year.
after work clothes --
Personal expenses - 80 IL per year 25 for children
get one book /yr
gifts - pesach (silverware - pot according to choice)
50th birthday get gift
every 2nd yr go somewhere for [illegible] paid for recreational home. 1 wks part of vacation
every year - 2 wks every year
gifts from outside - OK small ones

10- What connection in MOSAD between children & parents -
Go home Wed nite
Sat " Mon home.
arrange for parents visits.

11 - Do they have main dining room etc. at Mosad.
Its just like kibbutz for children.

Dania questions continued

12* Why do the children look up so much to high school kids.
Many levels of looking up - different - away from home.

13 - What happens if child decides to leave --
Try to convince them - if doesn't work then sad but can't do anything I have done this

Have you thought of having Univ. here so wont have to go away
Can't afford it - have through high school which is more than most for higher education send those who are needed.

14 + Do you have trouble with people not working as hard as others !! Shirking ??
45 - 7 hrs
50 - 6 hrs.

Some work more than they should !!
Public opinion is a powerful lever - if it doesn't work then the person doesn't have a place in the kibbutz - if extreme brought up to meeting

How about people like artists who can work in their profession which is fun or guests who work here
They are our guests & we encourage them

15- What is the red flag -
represents socialism - Equality of living -
classless society - land held together -
other resources . no speculation in land .

16- How about dates - steady
not customary to break away
Have party at Mosad .

NAMES

YONA YANAI
CHANA
ORNA , GIORA
SARA + SHIMON AVIDAN + DAPHNA
EHUD Reiter
AVRAM FINE
SHIFFRAH
Dov vardi (neighbor)
Joseph Wolfand

Acropolis Friday July 7 - the massing on
the hill is fantastically organized - what is interesting is the
asymetry altho' the buildings themselves are symetrical - the
approach is a winding devious thing & then when you
finally pass through the propylaea & arrive the parthenon is <u>not</u>
on axis - a fine growing experience of spaces.

Fontana Trevi - Tuesday
Rome - July 11th

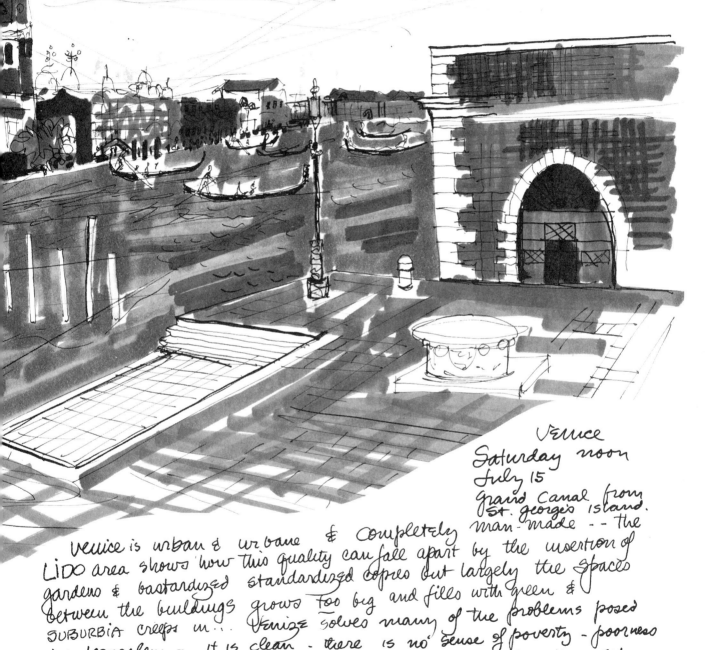

Venice
Saturday noon
July 15
grand Canal from
St. george's Island.

Venice is urban & urbane & completely man-made -- the LIDO area shows how this quality can fall apart by the insertion of gardens & bastardized standardized copies but largely the spaces between the buildings grows too big and fills with green & SUBURBIA creeps in... Venize solves many of the problems posed by Jerusalem - it is clean - there is no sense of poverty - poorness mebbe (but not poverty) & the public spaces including the great one at San Marco give a sense of measure & tempo & place. AND of course NO AUTOMOBILES The sound is great!

LOT No 2
25c

DO
NOT
ENTER

ONE WAY

NO
LEFT
TURN

Home again
Home again   — July 22.61
Sat morning 6:30 L.A. waiting
for flight to San Fran.

The Community ~~and~~ as Earth Sculpture

Sunday Sept 10, 1961
with in Camp
Tucker

I am sitting, as I write this article, at the bottom of a small canyon cut deep in into the core of the surrounding California hills by spring-fed streams. It is late in summer and the water is down now to a trickle. ~~where~~ In the spring this was a roaring River. now it is a small quiet unobtrusive little rill hard to see and barely audible as it runs over rocks and quietly under leaves and fallen branches. Down in the canyon in the deep shade there are redwoods and bay trees and alder and woodwardia fern. Moss carpets the ground and the lichens hang from the rocks. Up above - above where the canyon starts the sere dry California hills lie exposed to the hot golden sun - the tawny grasses shimmer, the chapparral is crackling dry, and the sage brush the buckeye leaves have already dried up and are dropping to the ground.

It is hard to realize now that this little stream has made the difference - has cut into the rocky hillsides and slowly, quietly worn down the rock and sculptured it into its new form. This Earth sculpture has been going on for a long time, for centuries. It has gone on so slowly that it has, in process, established its own patterns its own environment and achieved a wonderful ecological balance - earth - plants and animals.

Downstream there is the remains of an old logging trail and along it are some ancient redwood cabins, long abandoned, which served the logging crews for shelter & chuck houses They too have merged now into the forest floor - the lichen & moss have covered them over, the shape hooves have crumbled and it is almost difficult to distinguish these from the native forest so cosy are they with it.

Early communities too had this quality of identity with their natural environment. When men moved out of caves into houses of their own building they naturally used the materials at hand baked clay adobe, rocks, wood. And working slowly with their hands. with small inefficient tools they hacked and pushed at the earth to shape it slightly and slowly. As each succeeding house was built it, in turn, responding to its materials and the slow process of human-helped erosion added house next to house to form a community.

And these communities inevitably aquired that wonderful sense of organic growth & unity — that remarkable sense of inevitability which gives them an, alive, almost biological, quality. They relate magnificently to their sites, they are almost parts of them. The roads wind narrow between the houses just wide enough for people and animals to pass by & reach their homes. Since all had to be done by hand the least possible was done, the hills were left ungraded & each house tucked in next to its neighbor hardly disturbing the profile of the hill. The materials came from the site & so they too had a feel of the place. The whole, after a time, achieved a kind of ecologically visual balance which gave it the same organic quality as the canyon the same feeling of slow natural processes as the stream, the same rightness which happens when inexorable happenings give form to natures materials. On a small scale the arab village, the medieval town, the Italian hill town are as beautiful to be in and generate much the same quality of visual experience as a walk through a deep forest. The processes which generated the two are similar and so the qualities of visual experience, which they give remain similar. Forms evolved from similar processes and the responses of participation are related.

63

* But now our communities arise in different ways and our tools & processes are different. Our scale has changed. Our tempo has changed. Our purposes have changed.

Communities no longer grow — they are built — often all at once — houses by the thousands.

Materials now are manufactured — not hewn from the site

Tools are no longer hands but bulldozers, tractors, carryalls and great earthmoving equipment which can move mountains in days which used to take centuries

~~Our purposes~~

Community scale has changed — roads penetrate and disintegrate communities the numbers of people who live together has grown enormously — houses march on endlessly in never-ending rows.

The organic quality of communities has been lost — the great scars in the native landscape — the ugly utility poles, the insensitive imperative of the 50 foot lot aligned automatically alongside of a pseudo curving over-wide road deface the earth.

There is no longer any sense of organic growth & we have lost any relationship between the natural processes of earth sculpture and community growth.

Elements of a natural landscape
on a walk up 'Camp Tucker Canyon: Sunday - Nov. 5, 1961

1- Unpredictable rhythms -- as arrangements thru'
scatteration of trees...

2- Relatedness of things - colors all related
in brown range. fallen leaves, tree bark - earth etc
shapes etc.

3- Small counter rhythms - leaves falling.
branches moving.

4- Sounds are quiet but persistent &
unpredictable within a configurative pattern —
as the stream moving over rocks.

5 - All edges are soft - they feel as though
they have become by being worn - not
created into a fixed edge.....

6- Evolvement by either addition or subtraction
of shapes -- ie: erosion shapes on the additive
shapes of growth (trees, leaves falling etc.)

7- Non-completion of spaces --- the spaces all
move into other spaces & are non-confined.

8- Variability of light - non-fixed & glowing..

9—— This environment is permissive. it enables you to come
in & participate on your own level in any way you see fit.
it does not impose many restrictions. of limitations but
not restrictions.

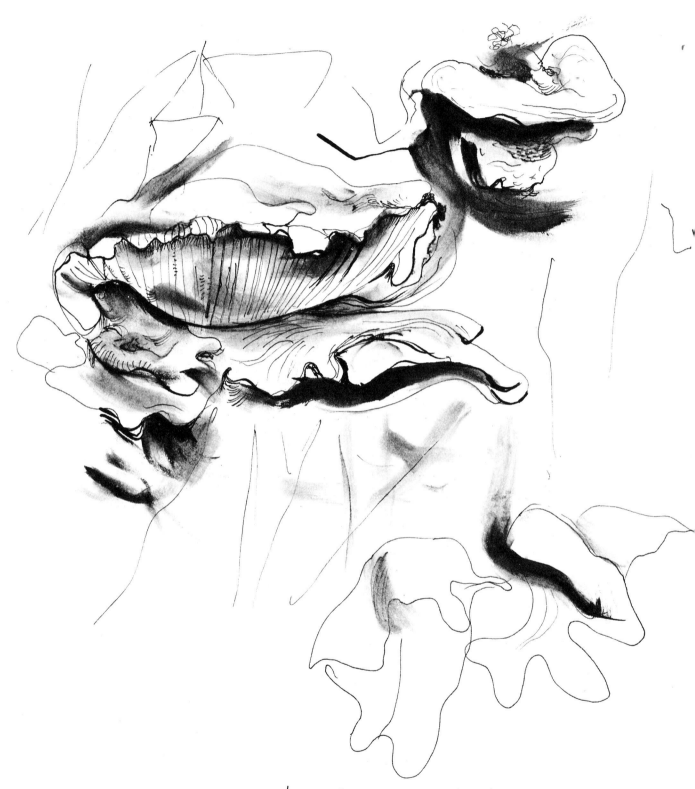

bract fungus on a bay tree
Camp tucker - Sunday Nov 5.

Rubus in woods
Sun May 6
1962

Telegraph Hill
March 1, 1962

THE ART OF ASSEMBLAGE

is important because it gives sharp focus to the idea that art & Life are the same tho' different facetted. It clarifies the fact that ART is Life sharpened, brought into focus, organized, concentrated, emphasized ... but the same elements !!

It is particularly meaningful to anyone designing for environment becuz it makes clear the breakdown of "ART for Arts" sake as a separated function - just as it breaks down the difference between painting & sculpture. Here one sees the ordinary cast-offs of our civilization concentrated in space & Time into organized "things" which one can call works of Art only because of the "purpose" behind their creation. i.e. the creation is in the act of putting them together the process and not in the Technique or the manufacture of the elements which already exist.

How important this is for us to understand - the simplest elements of a machine-made civilization put together excitedly into "evocative "things". These can go beyond the smallness of these museum oriented works to our real environment - Land - buildings - freeways - the mobiles (automobile etc etc. Nor should we stop there - Theatre - why in a building or a special place? - Out in the world - in plazas in streets in the market place - as in medieval times - the Passion Plays - Art enriches life not as decoration applied or even as specially designed & functional but as a heightening of Life's Processes.

or True Art vs. applied Art.

The artists function becomes one then of seeing &
through seeing to realize. possibilities of new juxtapositions
of new arrangements of new relationships and to bring them
to our attention through his art.

He needs to work free — without the dead weight
of responsibility which threatens the freedom of designers working
at "responsible" levels of government - bridge designers, or
architects or planners who have too much at stake to take
way out chances as can an artist who has only himself to
gamble & risk. He is our laboratory. If he misses we
gain - if he succeeds we gain. The only time we lose is if
he doesn't try—or tries shallow.

(We should do something about Sequiros. is there a
fund to contribute to or write letters through - find out!

notes on a flight to Seattle to check
world Fair Garden -- March 18-1962

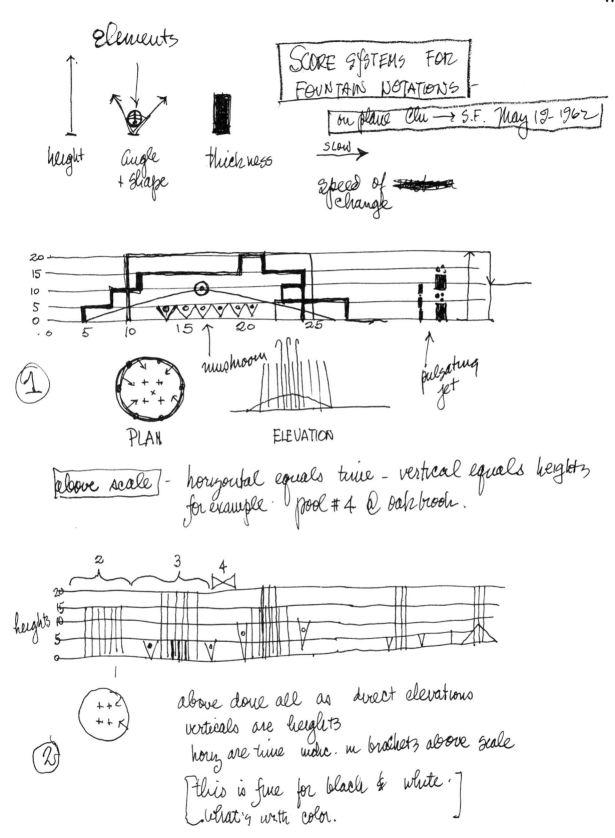

Elements

height

Angle + Shape

thickness

SCORE SYSTEMS FOR FOUNTAIN NOTATIONS —
on plane flu → S.F. May 12- 1962

slow

speed of change

mushroom

PLAN   ELEVATION

pulsating jet

1

above scale — horizontal equals time — vertical equals heights
for example · pool #4 @ oakbrook.

2   3   4

heights

2

above done all as direct elevations
verticals are heights
horiz are time indic. in brackets above scale

[this is fine for black & white.]
what's with color.

72

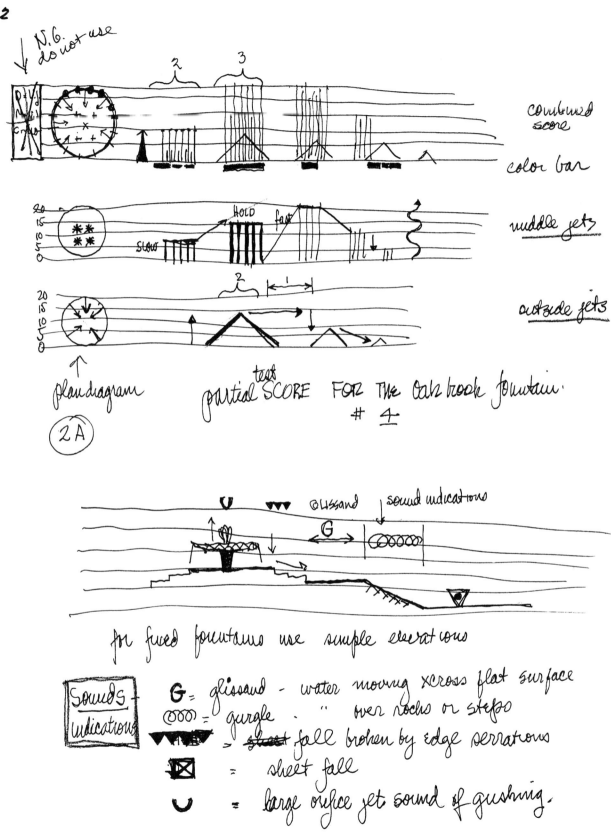

combined
score

color bar

middle jets

outside jets

plan diagram

partial test SCORE FOR THE Oak brook fountain.
4

2A

@lissand   sound indications

G

for fixed fountains use simple elevations

Sounds indications

G = glissand - water moving xcross flat surface
(OOO) = gurgle   "   over rocks or steps
▼▼▼ = ~~sheet~~ fall broken by edge serrations
⊠ = sheet fall
∪ = large orifice jet sound of gushing.

PLAN FOR A 45 MINUTE
ENVIRONMENT

May 30-62

✠ ˑ *fixed points*
⊞ *start*
⸬ GROUPS
🌀 *random*
↑↓ *semi - random*

⸺ *audience*
—*— " stop*
— — — *slow*

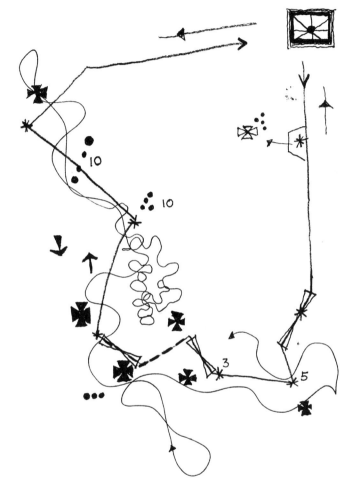

🔲 *level change*

3 — *time at fixed pts*

The score for each element must be
developed separately - see next page.

➡ * use audience in 5 groups of 15 each
leaving starting point every 5 MIN.
try also going in opposite directions

EXTENDED Section for
a 45 Minute Environment

May 30-1962
Memorial Day.

dancers workshop
composition class
with Ann Halprin

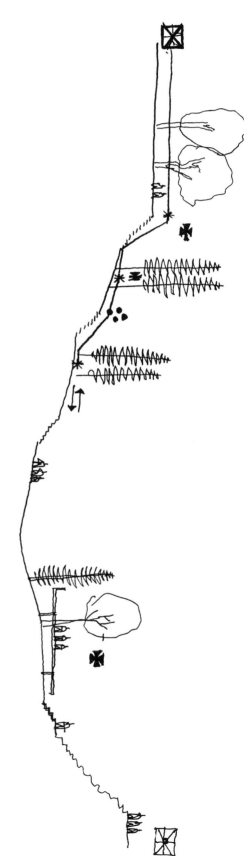

EXTENDED   SECTION...

Notes on the Ghiradelli Center For Bill Roth

June '62

It's quite clear that much of the old brick stuff should
stay. But some should come out !!!!

do
restaurant
in tower

outdoor
dining on roof
of existing office bldg.
next to tower - Enclose with
GLASS

PLAZA

balustrades

view

Exaggerated
existing
grade

North
POINT Street

arcaded shops
along street

SHOPS

ARCADE

view

IN TO
PARKING

SHOPS

ARCADE

street level

Parking

Parking

30' wide

block
of beach
street if
possible

PARKING

BEACH
STREET

access will be possible also from side streets.

Section (no scale)

The box factory should be removed as should the one story wings between
the old factories.

A great plaza at the upper level should be developed —
around it a "BEEHIVE OF EXCITEMENT" with several

layers of shops — all connected with each other by ramps and stairs from different levels ... ✓ this way

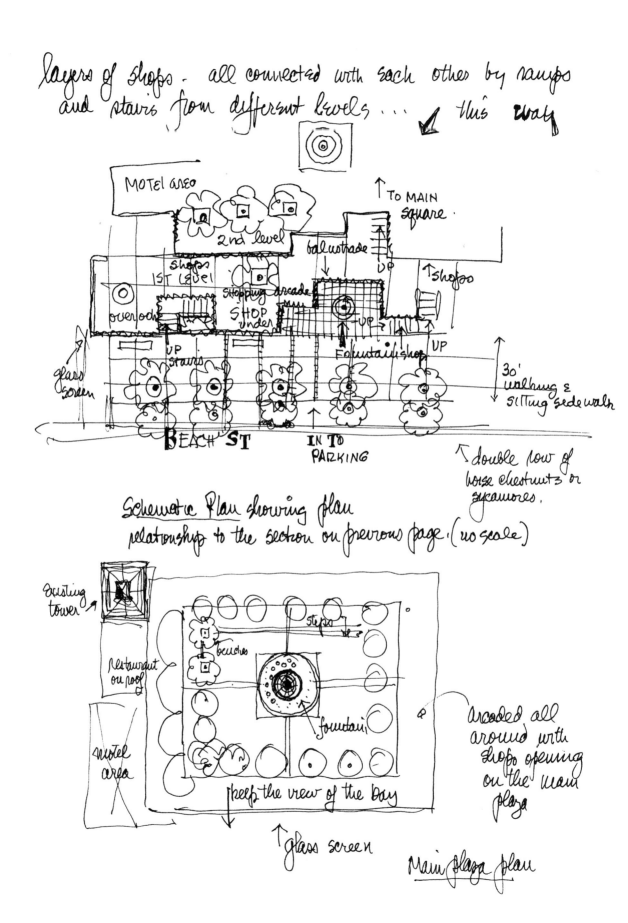

MOTEL area

2nd level

↑ TO MAIN square.

shops 1st level

balustrade

↑ UP

↑ shops

overlook

shopping arcade
SHOP under

↑ UP

UP stairs

fountain shop

UP

30' walking & sitting sidewalk

glass screen

BEACH ST

INTO PARKING

↑ double row of horse chestnuts or sycamores.

Schematic Plan showing plan relationship to the section on previous page. (no scale)

Existing tower →

steps

benches

Restaurant on roof

fountain

motel area

arcaded all around with shops opening on the main plaza

↓ keep the view of the bay

↑ glass screen

Main plaza plan

Parking is a major problem but since there is about a 30' break across the site several layers of underground parking can be developed! - see section - & these can also be made accessible from both side streets

The Beach street facade must be set back about 30' for a handsome promenade with trees, benches & sidewalk cafés - but not in a single line - set backs - interwoven together - see plan sketch.

III think a motel - very good one would be marvellous here - urban - urbane - lots of things to do - shopping, restaurants, an off-beat theatre - avant garde painting & sculpture on the plaza - rotating exhibits - I'd come & stay for a weekend myself!

BEACH

MARITIME

AQUATIC PARK

Beach street could be cut off to thru' traffic & become a pedestrian mall for walking & promenading with arches of lights etc. & flags.

I suggest buying the Dr Pepper site for additional parking, which probably would be needed if a motel & all the other facilities are developed at Ghirardelli Center.

Bishop Pass
from chocolate peak.
aug '62

Notes for campfire discussion - Margaret Lake
Back Camp
Sierra Club.... aug.'62

Aesthetics of the Sierra

appeal at different levels :—

ⓐ picturesque - photos by Ansel & Cedric
Wright + painter

ⓑ structural - the great shapes. ∿Ⲙ

ⓒ formal - re: sense of form -
boulders, rocks, rock faces
striations

ⓓ painterly - interrelations - patterns of
streams, grasses against rocks
shadows.
Color - subtle but exciting

ⓔ Sounds -   Streams
(as musician)   tinkles
roars, symphonic

ⓕ landscape -   rocks, grasses. etc.
trees, driftwood etc.

ⓖ choreographic - the movement, the
tension between objects

ⓗ COMPOSITION - our sense of composition
arrived at thru observation
of inevitable processes.

forest floor
Sunday - Mar 3
1963

The essential purpose of design is to create the possibilities for events to happen.

The limited qualities of perfection in design is that it is then fixed. No more can happen. It is ended. Anything added or subtracted from a perfect design demeans it & lessens its impact.

On the other hand an imperfect design accepts change & is enhanced by it.

By imperfect I mean incompleted.

Incompletion allows for addition or subtraction which enables a person to feel a part of it.

The static complete design can only be seen from outside, viewed as if through a viewer. A person cannot feel part of it because it does not need his participation.

A garden in which all is fixed is limited in time & space and humanity. I want a garden which is enhanced by chance occurrences which is enriched by weeds & suckering growth & the changing patterns of sunlight & shade & the branch falling on the terrace. It is better because I am a part of it.
It is not finished.

Sunday. March 24.

SEA RANCH

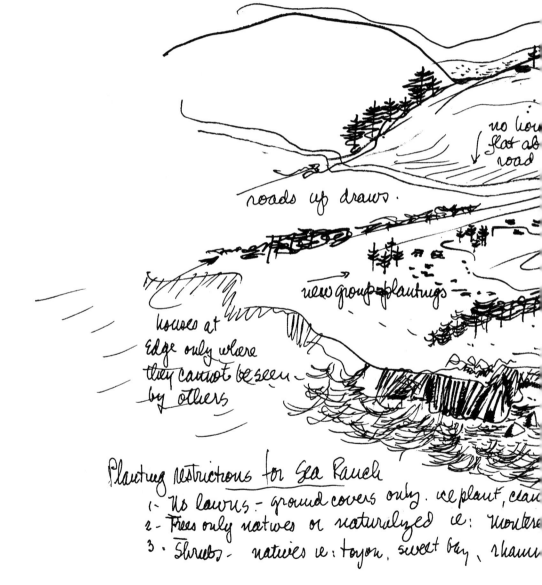

no hou
flat ab
road

roads up draws.

new group plantings

houses at
Edge only where
they cannot be seen
by others

Planting restrictions for Sea Ranch
1. No lawns - ground covers only. we plant, clau
2. Trees only natives or naturalized ie: Montere
3. Shrubs - natives ie: toyon, sweet bay, rham

1063

keep houses back
from ridge face
so only silhouette
can be seen

Riding trails ↑ no roads up face

Architectural restrictions —

These are harder to establish

1- Stable of archt's? — no review
2- Materials?
3- submissions; to arch. commission

between Anza & Balboa check the Stone pines
on East side. should be saved.
utilities are underground here! very nice things.

14 lanes @ transition point - WOW!!

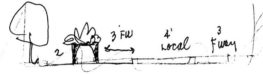

Anza will be closed.

Possible at transition.
The transition will be extremely
difficult to handle.

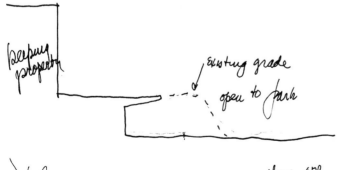

keeping property

existing grade
open to park

alternates at Fulton

X lose prop

these are
Atlantic cedars

POSSIBLE cantilever
sections along FULTON.

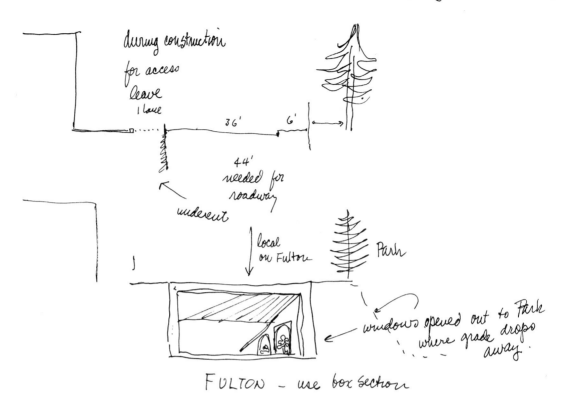

during construction
for access
leave
1 lane

3 6'   6'

44'
needed for
roadway

undercut

local
on Fulton

Park

windows opened out to Park
where grade drops
away.

FULTON — use box section

At the end near Civic Center there is a great shot
of the Civic Center which must be capitalized on—.

FERRY PARK   on trip to Dallas
Oct 3 · 63

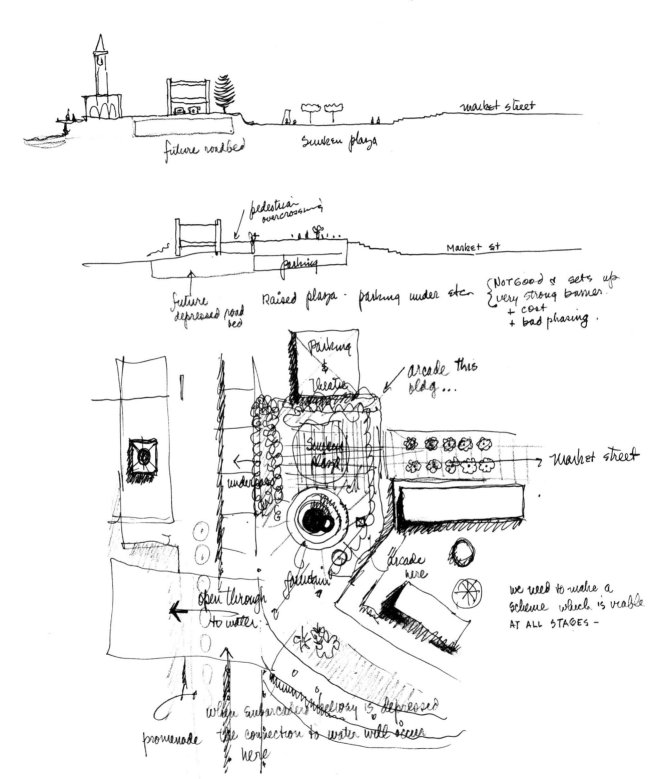

market street

future roadbed   Sunken plaza

pedestrian overcrossing

Market St

parking

future depressed road bed   Raised plaza - parking under etc.   { Not good & sets up } Every strong barrier
+ cost
+ bad phasing.

Parking & Theatre   arcade this bldg...

Sunken Plaza   Market street

underpass

fountain   Arcade here   we need to make a scheme which is viable AT ALL STAGES −

Open through to water

When Embarcadero freeway is depressed the connection to water will occur here

promenade

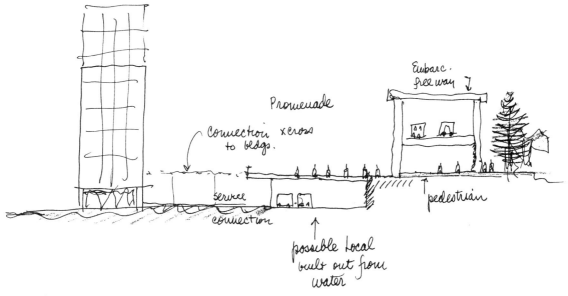

Promenade

connection xcross
to bldgs.

Embarc.
freeway

service
connection

possible Local
built out from
water

pedestrian

Possible Future traffic pattern for Embarcadero —

coit tower

where this now dead ends
& can cut over to Sansome
& go thru telegraph hill
as arcaded open sided tunnel
& then duck under Bay St

open sides

Arizona Landscape - 37,000' -
trip to Dallas Oct 3-63

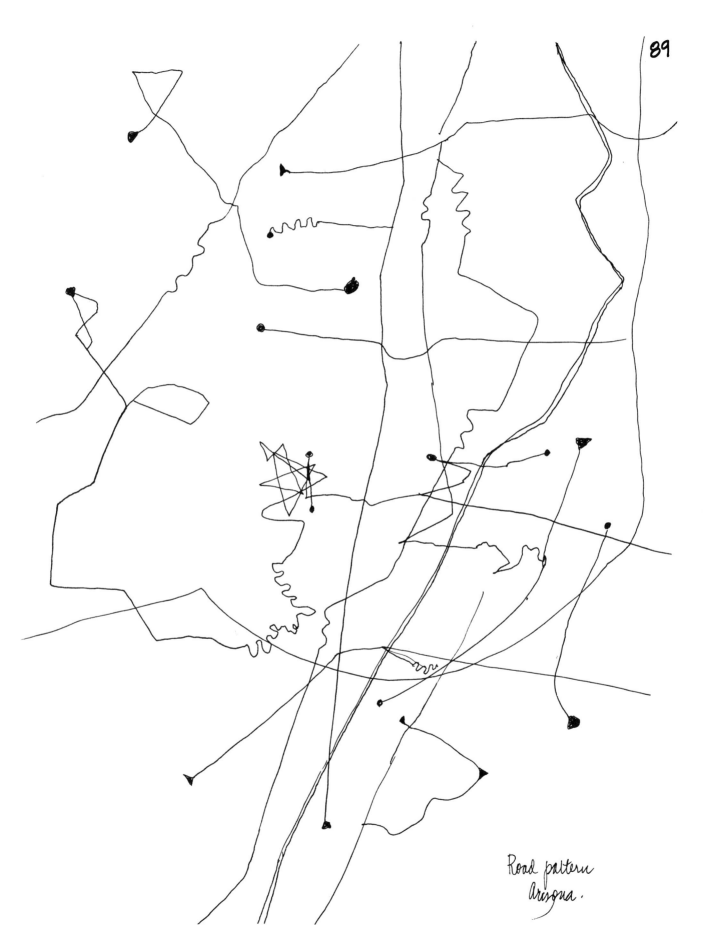

89

Road pattern
Arizona.

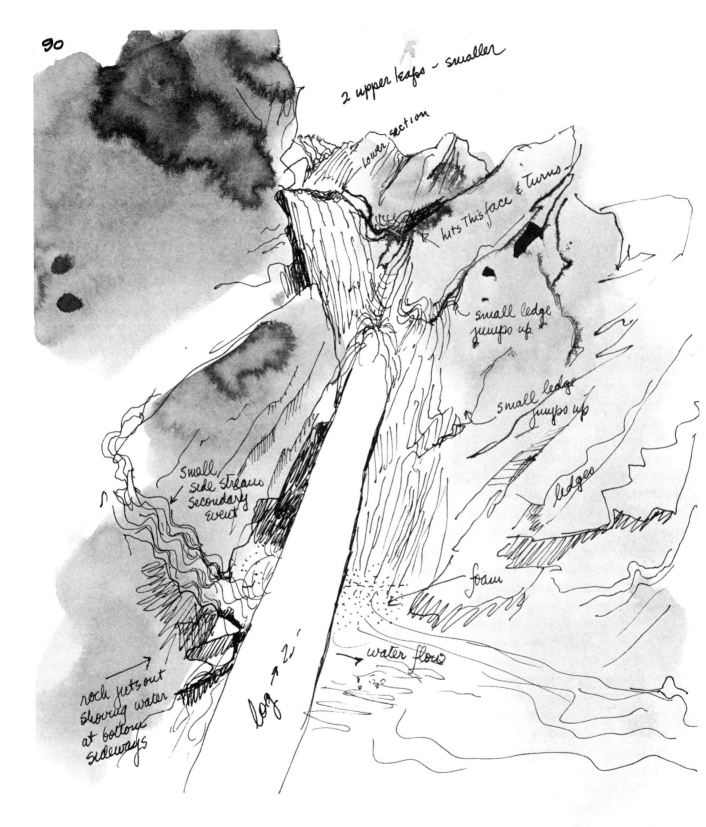

90

2 upper leaps - smaller

lower section

hits this face & turns

small ledge
jumps up

small ledge
jumps up

ledges

small
side stream
secondary
event

foam

rock juts out
shoving water
at bottom
sideways

log ↑ 2'

water flow

Halprin
North Fork
aug 1964

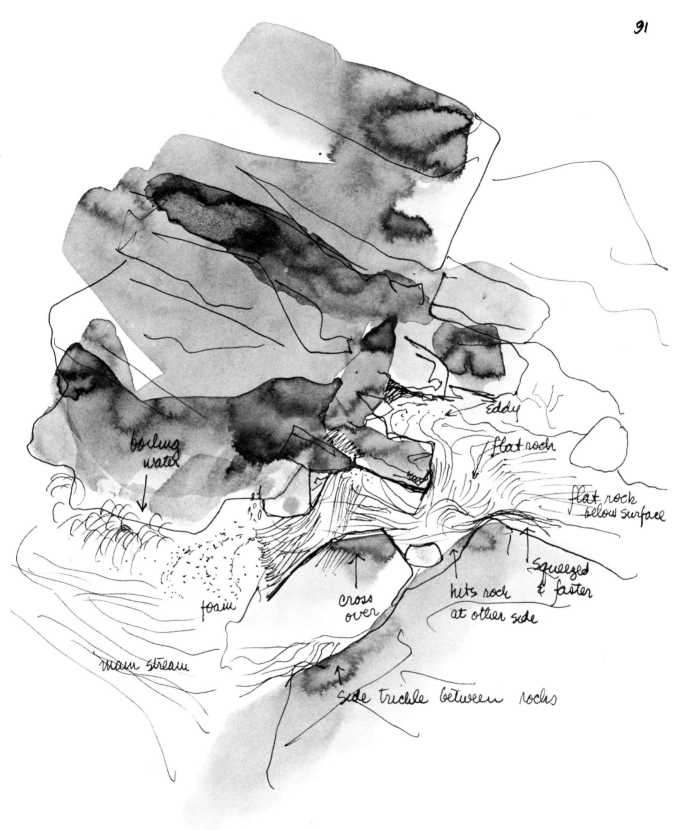

boiling
water

Eddy

flat rock

flat rock
below surface

foam

cross
over

hits rock
at other side

Squeezed
& faster

main stream

side trickle between rocks

Halprin

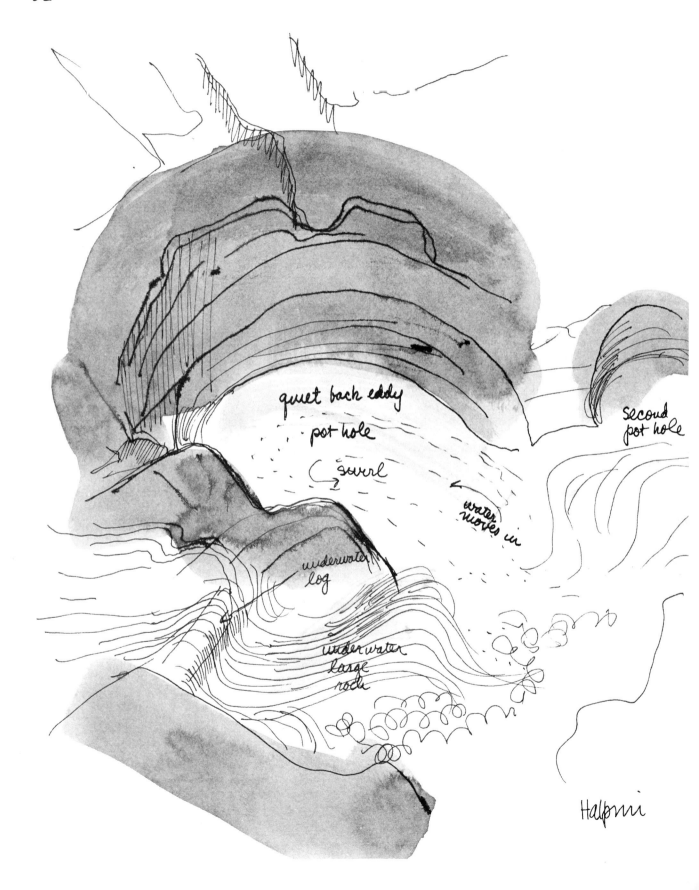

quiet back eddy

pot hole

swirl

water moves in

second pot hole

underwater log

underwater large rock

Halprin

leap

bounce

bubble

Eddy

surge

Eddy

boil

glide

leap

Halprin

deep fissure

flat cleft face

corbelled base

Scree & grass

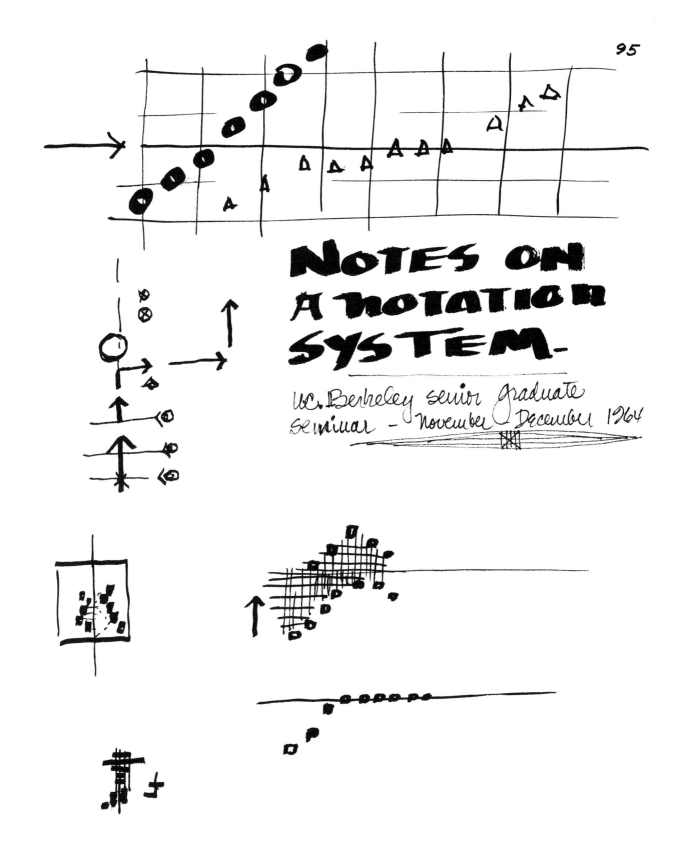

NOTES ON A NOTATION SYSTEM.

U.C. Berkeley senior graduate seminar — November - December 1964

speed of motion

0   10   20   30   feet

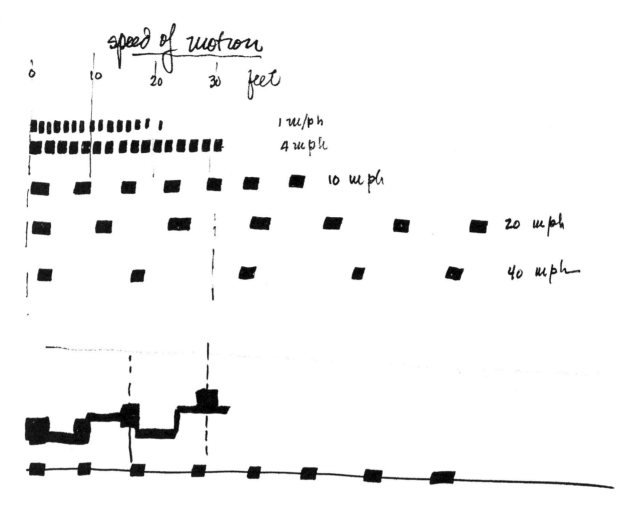

1 m/ph

4 mph

10 mph

20 mph

40 mph

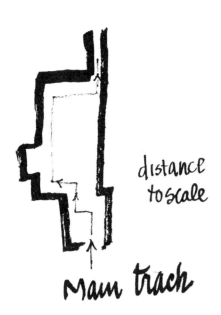

distance
to scale

Main track

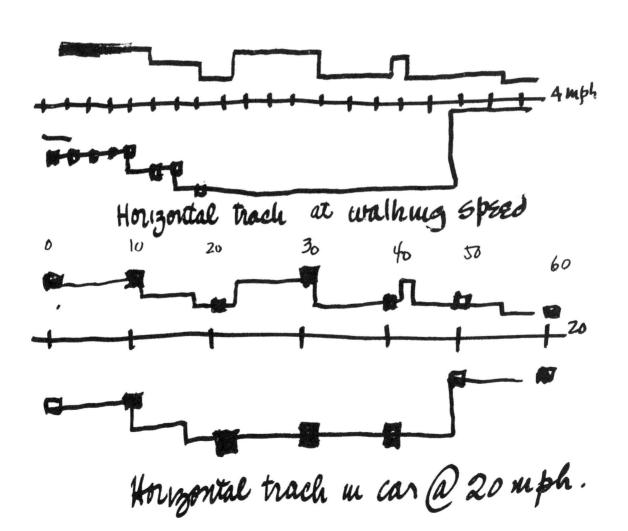

Horizontal track at walking speed

4 mph

0   10   20   30   40   50   60

20

Horizontal track in car @ 20 mph.

Philosophic base

   design for motion should ∴ have new
1   system to describe motion

 RENAISSANCE

 modern

 medieval

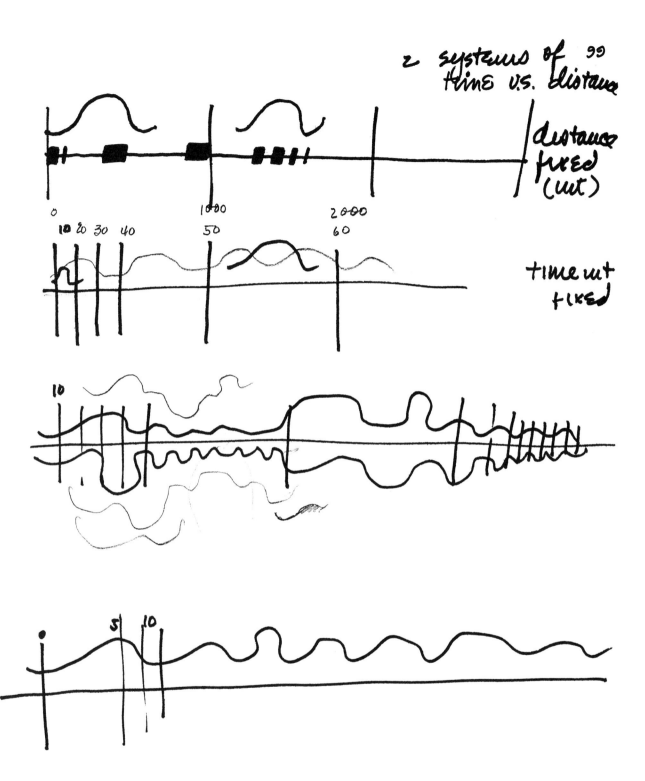

2 systems of time v.s. distance

distance fixed (unt)

0   1000   2000

10 20 30 40   50   60

time unt fixed

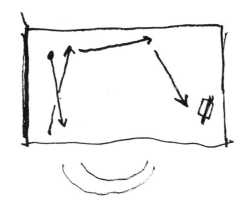

notation of
a dance motion

Plan
ie: main track

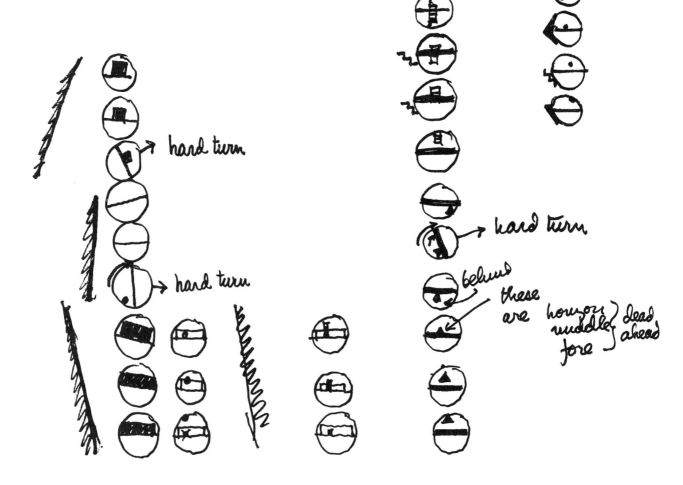

hard turn

hard turn

hard turn

behind
these
are horizon
middle
fore
dead
ahead

a theatre
movement for
Pat Hickey

2W

work out fixed
Symbols

etc

D.D.D

S

AALeith   John

S = sit
☰ = stairs

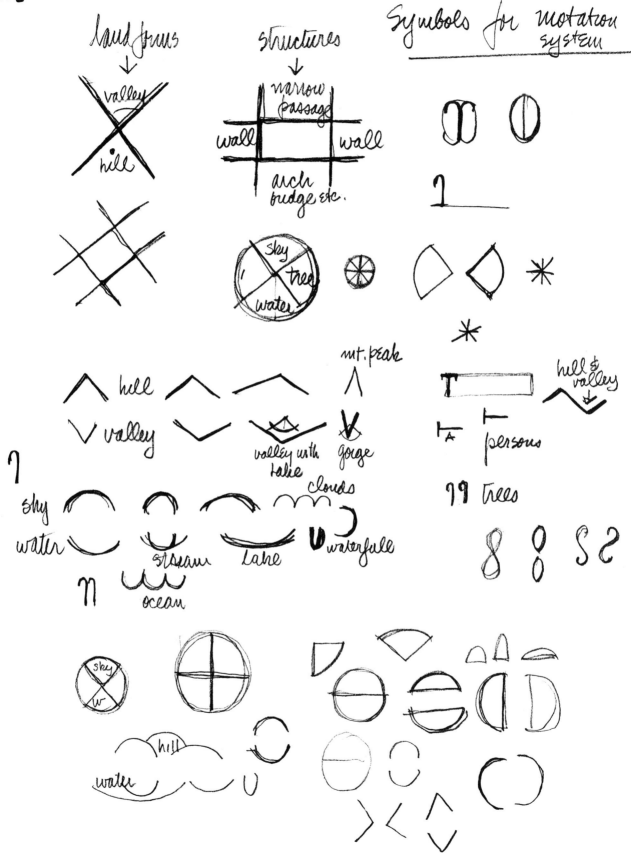

Symbols for motation system

land forms → valley / hill

structures → narrow passage / wall / wall / arch bridge etc.

mt. peak

hill
valley
valley with lake
gorge

persons

99 Trees

hill & valley

sky
water
stream
lake
clouds
waterfall
ocean

sky
tree
water

sky
w

hill
water

combinations of
symbols

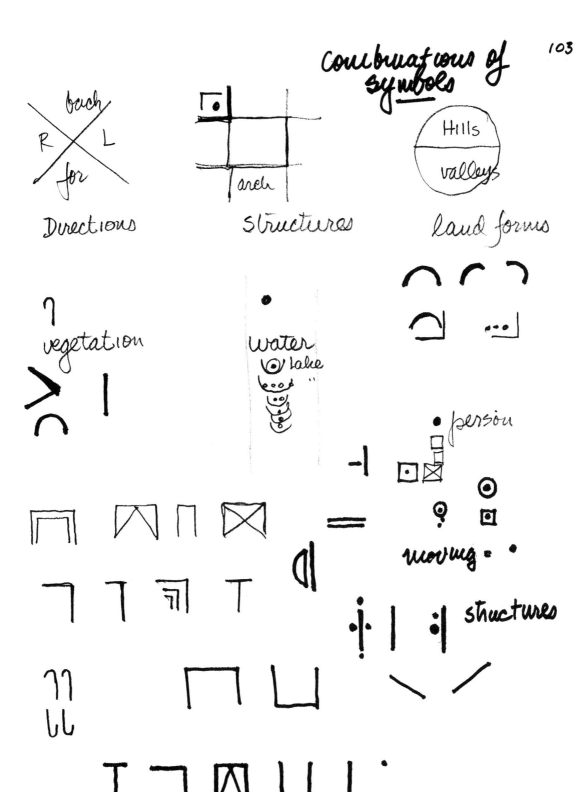

Directions

Structures

land forms

vegetation

water
lake

person

moving =

structures

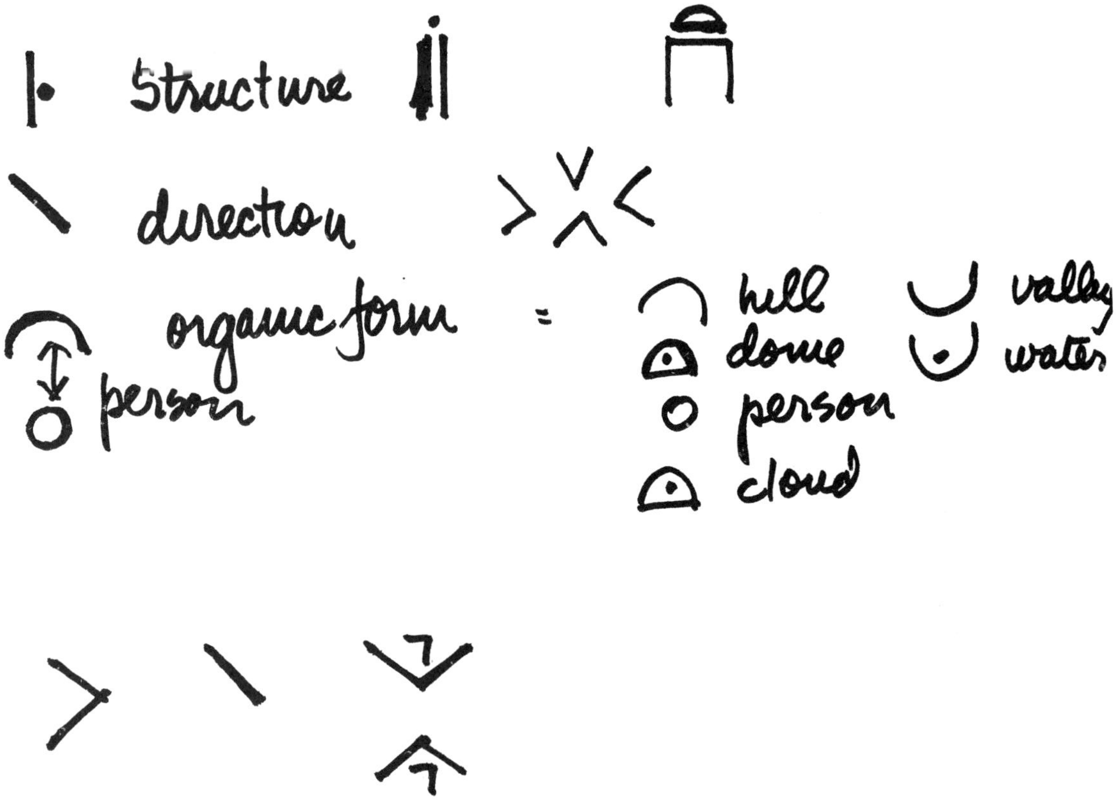

|•	structure
\	direction
	organic form
person

hill
dome
person
cloud

valley
water

A city is like a biological community -
an ecosystem - based on natural foundations.
Soils - climate - food place - a series of
complex interactions in
which a long period of initial jockeying
goes on - young - adolescent maturity.
derived from processes

CLIMAX - community - a stable
form - fixed no's & types of inhabitants
a balance is established of plants & animals
all in equilibrium.

But a biological community never
reaches real equilibrium - in the newer view
of ecosystems the concept of DISCLIMAX occurs
where continuous change occurs operating on
stability to effect a continuous process.

cities are like biologic communities
in that they too achieve a form of stability
but also are continually in process or they
become nuisances - VENICE
The big difference between the purely
biologic process of plant & animal communities
& cities is that they are completely at the

mercy of memorable forces & unaffected by
judgements of value or choice. In the control
of cities we have the opportunity to effect choices as
change occurs.

The need to differentiate between
valuable change — what to change to & what
to hold on to ———

~~a city is there for the people to live in.~~
" " " a biologic phenomenon and a work of art
& the 2 are similar —

change | 1- <u>Sense of place</u> - <u>Skyline</u>° - <u>natural geography</u>
HongKong — Jerusalem — Florence
Rome - Paris - S.F.

"FIXED"? 2- <u>Sense of neighborhoods</u> - HongKong etc.
density - high rise - low etc.

change | 3- <u>Transportation</u> — heirarchy - Venice
mass transit
cars - freeways including absorptive capacity
pedestrians (areas of preservation) college campuses
or worlds fairs?

4 - <u>Waterfronts</u> - their value
Paris-Rome - HongKong - Rotterdam

5 - Open spaces

6 - Streets - hierarchy of streets

7 - The art of Cities as sculpture - Ginza - S.F.
New York - vitality

But the city is simply part of the ecology
of a region of which it is the center ———

      Sierra
      Big Sur
      Sea Ranch
      Bay

Some of these can allow for change as
part of the total community structure —

ⓐ Some fill but mostly not

ⓑ   "   habitation — villages in the country
               {as against suburbs

ⓒ But some need complete preservation — insulation
   from access.   Sierra
           alps , (Jackson Square)

ⓓ need for preservation of good farmland.

108

architects have always designed things not processes

we realise the world thru' our bodies . . . . . .

When start have "wants" & Rage .
Continuous response to his demands.
Establish breast - face = trust - -

As his physiology develops so does his reactions - -
Toilet training = control & order

Redwood stump
with moss –
Feb 28- 1965

Notes & thoughts for lecture to Engineers

1- A work of engineering is based on a single
purpose - bridge to span a void. no special
concern for peripheral or secondary purposes - ie:
views from bridge - silhouette on skyline - blockage
of views etc.

Solution of a single problem - usually of structure

Unilateral idea. 1:1 relationship

2. A work of architectural design does the above &
in addition worries about function in human sense,
proportion, impact on
the viewer + other peripheral purposes such as
relationship to other structures etc.

It may have a concern for symbolic purposes -
religious feelings, strives consciously to involve
the viewer, to make him "enjoy" it in the same
sense as all works of art -- be related to it.

3- A work of environmental design goes beyond and
concerns itself with the whole impact on its
environment at present and in the future: the
environmental impact can be very minor - small
footbridge, or extremely involved - freeway
interchange - freeway itself etc. within
the landscape. It includes engineering &
architectural design but extrapolates from them
into a multiplicity of "purposes" including
value judgements, even moral judgments.

At its best it is a conscious form of human
oecology.

Examples: (not in order)

1 - Bridges: Richmond - silhouette
rail - blocks view

g.g.B - silhouette
rail permits view

Seine -
Big Sur -

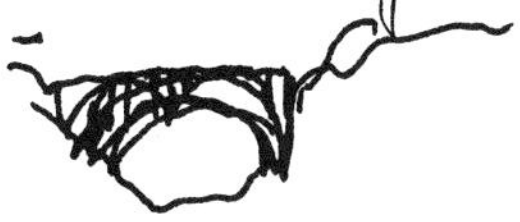

2 - Freeways

Hway 1 cuts
connecticut
oakland - Overpass.

3 - Transit Systems.

integration with the community.
urban - plazas. stations etc.
Country - linear parks - bicycle paths etc.

discussion with Bill Gilbert
re: Engineers lecture

1. traditionally engineering problems are presented with very specifically defined parameters.

↓ Load

no knowledge of origin or 3 dimensional quality
no perspective or model

2. 20-20 tunnel vision →

3. good - verrazano bridge

Engineers believe that if good structure that automatically makes it beautiful.
"Richmond bridge" for example.

Pressure - ultimate good is to make things as inexpensive as possible

make diff between engineers who are designing for arch - ie armatures which are covered over & "seen" structures such as bridges.

april '65

VISIT @ nite to Ghirardelli Square to "Crit" the night lighting -

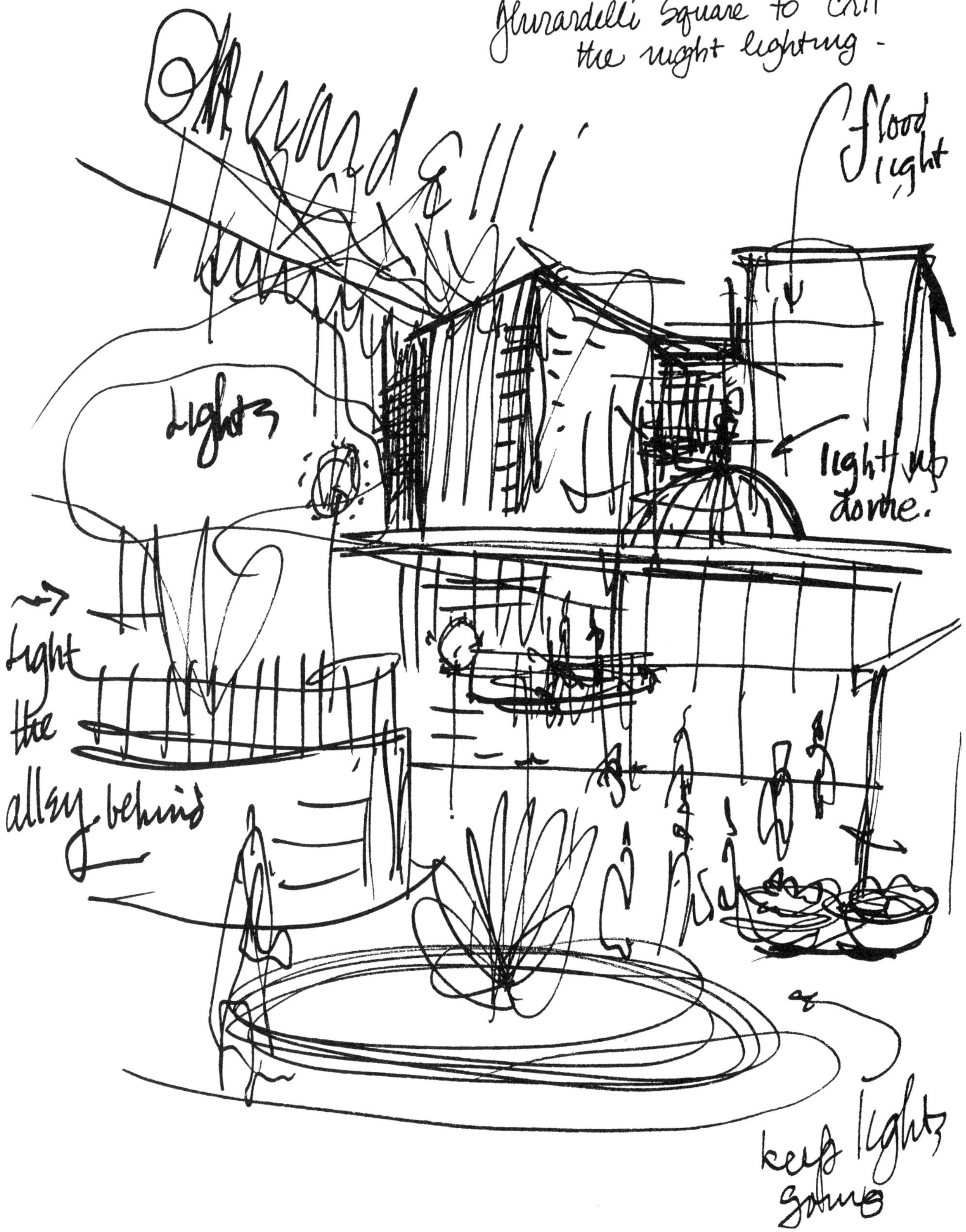
Ghirardelli
flood light
lights
light up dome.
light the alley behind
keep lights going

1. the cycle on the fountain is too
   quick — light sequences should
   stay on _much_ longer.

2. The building at end should stay
   lit (also the bookstore) even if it
   requires G. paying for it ————

OPEN

open thru'

light up behind
with all kinds of brightly lit events !!

Notes for article on Natural Sciences
article for student magazine @ Cal.

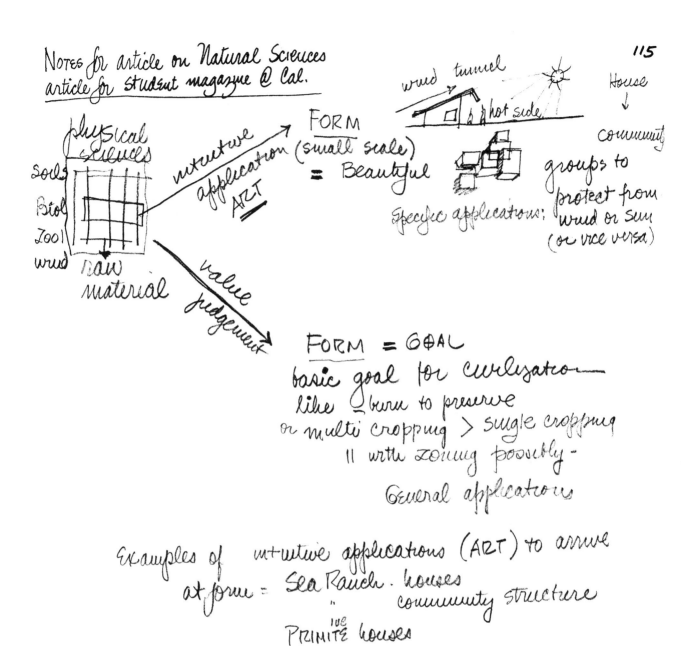

physical sciences

soils
Biol
Zool
wind

raw material

intuitive application ART →

FORM (small scale) = Beautiful

wind tunnel

hot side

Specific applications:

House ↓ community

groups to protect from wind or sun (or vice versa)

value judgement →

FORM = GOAL
basic goal for civilization
like to burn to preserve
or multi cropping > single cropping
|| with zoning possibly —
General applications

Examples of intuitive applications (ART) to arrive
at form = Sea Ranch. houses
" community structure
PRIMITIVE houses

Notes for Presidents Conference
on natural Beauty

~~Handsome~~ readily

Freeways can be designed for new cities or for new sections of older cities ~~by~~ as parkways whose characteristics are similar to freeways in the country ie: wide rights of ways, widely separated roadbeds and heavily screened verges.

However, when inserted into ~~the~~ older sections of densely built up urban cores where land values are high, existing architectural and urban values are important to preserve, and residential & commercial areas will be disrupted, freeway ~~#~~ design must find other solutions

add to # 6 -

Freeways should be built as part of a ~~total~~. community development - not unilaterally. If a freeway must pass through a city its design & construction must involve the total environmental redevelopment of the area through which it passes. To this end many levels of government as well as private enterprise must join forces to effect the complete redevelopment which should involve the buildings on our rights over freeways as well as the rebuilding of areas around it. Freeways can then take the lead etc etc

7. Freeways must be developed as part of a total transportation program in which mass transit & other techniques play a determining role.

8. The absorptive capacity for cars in a city must be determined. As a result of this evaluation adequate parking facilities to handle the absorptive capacity must be provided. and when these 2 factors are exceeded techniques for limiting further car-traffic must be established

118

log in garden
Sunday – June 20

I am having a terrible time trying to
compose the speech for the ASLA convention on
the 100ᵗʰ Anniversary of Landscape Architecture

I cannot bring myself to write prophetic words
"   "   "   "   "   " philosophic "

It seems so dull to have to spend the
time telling a group of people what they
already know, or already suspect. And if they
don't already know it then they should.

I don't particularly want to be "inspirational"
although I could make this kind of talk &
that is what they want

⟹   If the talk in itself could
be a liquid conversation — in which
nothing would be grasped.
——

On undesign
" the description of eventulism
" notation and its projection of
mobility as a determinant of
form

on the container v.s. the thing contained

on the banality of the "arrangement"
    of the physical environment.

on the order inherent in disorder.

on the ongoing qualities of design

on naturalism as a process

on goal-making as a form of ecology.

In the past year the following things
have really moved me : —

- Watts towers
    Disneyland
- Los Angeles freeways
    Harlyn Halvorsens experiments (in a horrible building)
- Sea ranch
- Astronaut in space movies
- tiger balm garden
- The Ginza (TOKYO)
- Parades and changes.

The Tiger Balm Garden

The whole garden is made of a kind of stucco - variously colored - after being there for even a few moments one feels as if the world has become metamorphosed and the most fantastic dreams have come true. These dreams, cast into human and animal shapes mount the hill in a series of tableaux each separate ~~from each other~~ but connected to each other by ramps and stairs which climb and pirouette and pass over & under each other through caves, past stalactites & stalagmites whose colors like the rainbow ooze and flicker in the varying light. ~~of~~

The tableaux, like phantasmagoria, are variously like congealed screams, like frightening nightmares or erotic dreams ~~congealed~~ ^fixed^ in time. The most beautiful maidens lie on the ground next to men disguised as monkeys. In separate rooms ^nude^ wrestlers accost each other and beyond an audience made up ~~of~~ unsavory characters watches forever the circus of Chinese ~~little~~ players.

Walls covered by ~~stucco~~ bas-reliefs tell the story of the 10 deadly sins each more venal than the next - each with its appropriate and bloody punishment and in a cave beneath the hill mermaids comb their hair and nude beauties beckon you on to unattainable fulfillment. Hours later the dreams linger and in retrospect one wonders what was imagined and what was real — what part of the garden represents your own dreams and which the dreams of the builder.

The Watts Towers

It takes a long time to find the watts towers which Simon Rodia built over a period of 35 years. Part of the difficulty is that they are buried in a simple neighborhood of small bungalows on 60 foot lots along a narrow street. There is nothing there to indicate an event —

You drive down a long street searching for the towers — there are several wrong turns — finally you make the right one and there they are.

The whole complex is on a tiny triangular lot facing a railroad track at the end of the street. It is surrounded by a 7' cement wall covered by tiles and broken bottles, pressed by shapes and figures while still wet so that their imprint is all over the wall. Inside the gate the world becomes immensely personal — the street disappears and the small space occupied by towers and cages, enclosures and strange shapes takes on the qualities of an enormous cityscape in ~~the~~ capsule. The wall from within ~~too~~ expands the scale. figures move about quietly as if in a quiet dream and the children climbing about within the towers seem like actors in a medieval passion play among the spires of the church.

The towers are not ~~structures~~ tall - 60-70 feet at most - but after a time, within the wall, dimensions change & the quality of height and of the structures built like intricate and encrusted spiderwebs grow enormous. The city within becomes more & more intense - a step represents an entire promenade and the colors of the tile envelop you. ~~walk~~ Floors are intricately patterned by the simplest devices of pressing shapes in the concrete - steps are emblazoned in tile, walls are less enclosures than modulators of tiny spaces - one walks among them as if in a dance and each turn becomes an event.

The views up through the intricate structures of the openwork towers are like looking at the rays of sun light diffused through a cloud.

The Sea Ranch

The Sea Ranch is a ten-mile stretch of rocky coastline 2½ hours north of San Francisco. This is an area of fog and wind of strong surf, of redwoods up on the ridges and hot sun by the Gualala river inland on the Andreas fault. Sea Ranch is being developed as a recreation community for people living in the S.F. Bay area — a place for hunting & fishing for summer homes and riding trails, for abalone and skin-diving, surfing, ~~and~~ ~~jassm~~ lying on the beach and poking around among the rocks.

A year of careful oecological studies revealed a great deal about the land which was not apparent at the start. It was found by ~~careful~~ precise meteorological & wind studies along the shore, that the wind could be controlled by particular types of architectural design — by slopes on rooves for example wind could be funneled up and over protected outdoor living areas, that by locating houses in the lee of existing wind rows calm zones 10 × the distance of the height of trees could be developed.

Up in the woods forestry practice was studied at length and a careful logging program was developed which thinned out weak trees, developed views and allowed sunlight into the forest floor. And a carefully organized program of controlled burns - removed accumulated litter from the forest floor - overcame the danger of hot disastrous fire and fertilized the valuable choked out understory of ferns and rhododendron.

Along the coastline the entire sea front has been left open by organizing housing into tight village-like clusters of houses and apartments so that each has its views - everyone has access to the coast and no wall of obstructive buildings fences in what has been left for everyone to enjoy. Common areas of green envelop the buildings and form a matrix for living.

Buildings are of wood & shingle - rooves follow the pitch and slope of the hills- seemingly grow out of the land on which they are built. The architecture and the land enhance each other and what has been planned is an environment in which man and nature, with mutual respect, look after each other in a biologically ordered way.

Parades and Changes

The theatre is our landscape....

we are a family of people who move through
this landscape, responding along with
our materials to a life situation.

Our materials are the colorful objects of every day
life - flags, bunting, hats, dresses, signs
symbols, benches, objects of all sorts.

we move ~~everyday~~ in a randomized way
among the objects which surround us
influenced by the light which shines on us,
the structures we encounter on our way,
the facades of buildings lining our paths.

we are involved in a process.
The process becomes the form.
What we touch upon in one evening's time
span is a series of eventful, meaningful, intense
relationships which the performer and audience
alike become a part of & which in everyday
life could take years to ~~observe~~ observe & experience.

The Los Angeles Freeways

In Los Angeles you never seem to say where you are going - you explain how to get there. First you take the Santa Anna Freeway - ~~when~~ after ~~you go~~ ~~the~~ 10 miles ~~you get~~ you change over to the ~~Anaheim~~ Santa Monica Freeway which you stay on for 15 miles and then turn onto the Anaheim freeway. Then you are there.

The great excitement is in the travel — a kind of free wheeling - free moving mobility in which the sense of motion and speed is important. The quality is like swimming with fins - the water buoys you up and the slightest effort propels you forward -- here the freeway is ~~the~~ the carrier - you push down the ~~accelerator~~ ~~pedal~~ and away you go - fast. Terraplaning over the land at tree top level - the rooves of houses below you - almost like flying.

Disassociated, encased in speed, nowhere to go but forward until in an involved imbraiding your freeway inunds and passes under over and around a beautiful and involved series of geometric ramps and overpasses under and over and _again_ away we go.

The Ginza. * * *

~~As may this day the ginza is not such a time~~

I remember the first evening I arrived in TOKYO.
I was met by the Japanese landscape architect
Tadachi. After we had bowed and spoken to
each other he asked me to join him in a drink.
This seemed pleasant and so we left the hotel
with some friends, for the Ginza. The streets at
the hotel were dark and narrow. But very soon
we got into a blaze of lights - not lights but
whole buildings designed to be light fixtures - whole
streets blazing with color, blinding - colorful,
moving tall towers looking like the inside of
a light bulb - brilliant.

All around, the streets were crowded with
young people moving through these streets as if
through a lightmobile - silhouetted ~~in their~~ against
the brilliance of the buildings. The light increased
ones sense of speed and excitement - the sound
of voices increasing with the foot-candles of brilliance
the whole scene became a cacophony of color
& light and sound and involvement.....

Down the side alleys the great signs hang
from the coffee houses and bars where up a

long staircase modern geishas welcome you in —
hold your hand — and, in the bar, giggle behind
their fingers.

The High Sierra

Last August up in the high Sierra ~~me~~ I climbed from our camp at 10.000 feet and struck out along a long series of uptilted planes of granite towards Mt. Ritter. The granite had been ~~scoured~~ by glaciers aeons ago and the sun slanting on the glacial polish made it look like burnished copper.

I was above timber line and, as I walked, the sound of the wind hung from the cliffs all around me and the waterfalls streaming down from the high glaciers cut ~~steps~~ in long uneven steps down the rock until they fell over the last cliff into the meadows far below.

It was quiet.
It " hard and peaceful.

Movies of the astronaut in space

These films taken of astronaut Miller outside
the space capsule seemed to me like the
quintessence of mans fancies - the accomplishment
of dreams - the ~~accomplishment~~ concretization
of esoteric symbols.

There - in a void of space, anchored only by
the distant image of the earth man tumbled about
~~glued to the universe~~
like ~~ancient~~ Icarus, ~~floating~~
        ancient
~~free~~ floating free but

Harlyn Halvorsen's Experiments

At the University of Wisconsin in the ugly moderne building of the Department of bacteriology Dr. Harlyn Halvorsen is pursuing studies on the characteristics of the genetic materials in paramecia. I asked him how close he felt he was getting to synthesizing life and he said quite close.

But then he said there was evidently going to be an issue of structure. By removing nuclei from one paramecium & inserting it into another he said we find that the ~~nucleus~~ original paramecium continues to develop in its own particular way. The nucleus apparently contains the necessary chemical elements for continued development but has no influence on its structural organisation

Though we may have been able within a very short time to synthetically create life we have no clues at the moment as to how to structure it.

The materials of life are close at hand.

But the order is a mystery.

Halp—
Sea Ranch
Store from road
June '65

fishtail stone shingles

clapboards horizontal

this distance not more than height of house ± 30'

rooves pitch in opposite direction

stagger back 4'

this house closes the view

square stones

fishtail slate roofing

white

blue

gray yellow

green

lilac bush

tree tan

green bushes

fence 5'

fence 5'

5' grass

fence

stairs up

20'

5'

tan

typical Norwegian street from Hotel Lindström Laerdal - aug 25 - 1965

Arrival from station into town center is
excellent. 20 minutes from town.

Town center same plan as Lincoln Nebraska

with some offsets

But question - should town center look like
shopping center. I think not - should have
street + separate areas for parks & plazas as in
old city.
The close in tall point blocks do not impinge at
all on the town center - mebbe & so scattered -
one would rather they did

playgrounds

view towards center
from the town house area.

The scheme seems very scattered with almost too much
green running through it. It would be very
dull & disorderly without the 3 dimensional quality
of the rolling ground, granite outcroppings & the
wonderful pines & birch trees.

VALLINGBY   Thursday Sept 2

Arrive by Subway under town center - in many
ways better than by elevated. As one approaches
town (on surface at this point) there is a
quality of skyline & "place" which one gets which is good

street

cars
here but
paving
same

← PIAZZETA

dark
L.T.
PIAZZA

up

streets↑

↓

theatre

up →

drive &
under
to
station

comm
bldg

↑
up from
the station

Church

tall
blocks

The quality of urbanity is much stronger here than at
Farsta — main square is <u>enclosed</u>. & there are
secondary spaces. There is a feeling of a plaza — not
just a shopping center and there seems room for
expansion. as they are in fact doing — the whole
thing is not locked into a completed scheme.

view of main
plaza

terrace housing

cars access

school

green sp

playing fields

underpass to town center

view North from town center
parking structure to terrace housing

142

Stockholm .. Dancer's workshop.....
rehearsal @ stadsteatern — parades & changes

3

SOUND
5 MIN

FLASHLIGHTS

25 MIN

+ VOCAL

REMOVE
PLASTIC

12 MINUTES.

3a instrument
3b environment

4

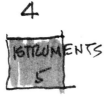

INSTRUMENTS

5

5

SOUND
w/
PLASTIC

overlaps

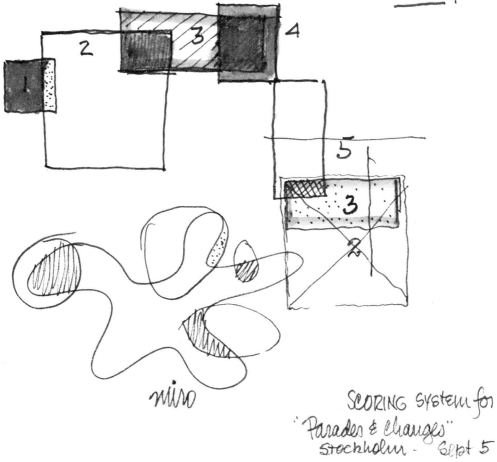

miro

SCORING SYSTEM for
"Parades & changes"
Stockholm - Sept 5

Choreographic plan

area designations

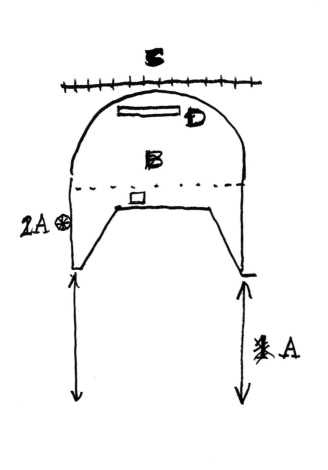

2A ✳

B

D

C

A

1 * 2 * 3 * 4 — Change designation to
A · B · C · D

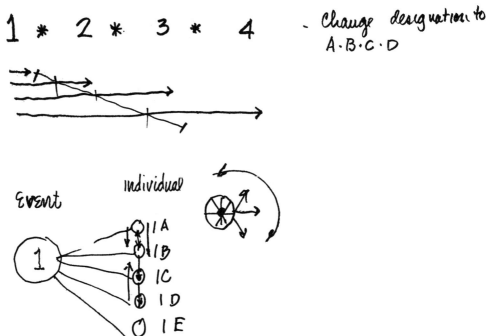

Event

Individual

1

1A
1B
1C
1D
1E

People Score '45

♯ Raua – 2A flashlights
4 instruments

✕ PAUL – 2 flashlights
3 ♭ plastic environment
5 plastic + sound

✳ LARY 2A
4
3 ♭
5

○ JANI 2c
4
3 ♭
5

⊙ DARIA 2A, 4, 3♭, 5

✸ KIM 2A 4, 3♭, 5

✛ JOHN – 2, 3♭, 5

‡ A.A. 2, 3♭, 5

⊕ ANN ~~striked out~~ 2A
3a

Υ FOLKE 1A.
5

---

1 | Υ
2 – | □ ✕ ✳ ○ ○ ✸ + ‡ ⊕
4 | □ ✳ ○ ○ ✸
3b | ✕ ✳ ○ ○ ✸ + ‡
5 | ✕ ✳ ○ ○ ✸ + ‡ Υ
2a | ⊕
2b | ⊕
3a | ⊕

TOTAL SCORE OF
Participants

146

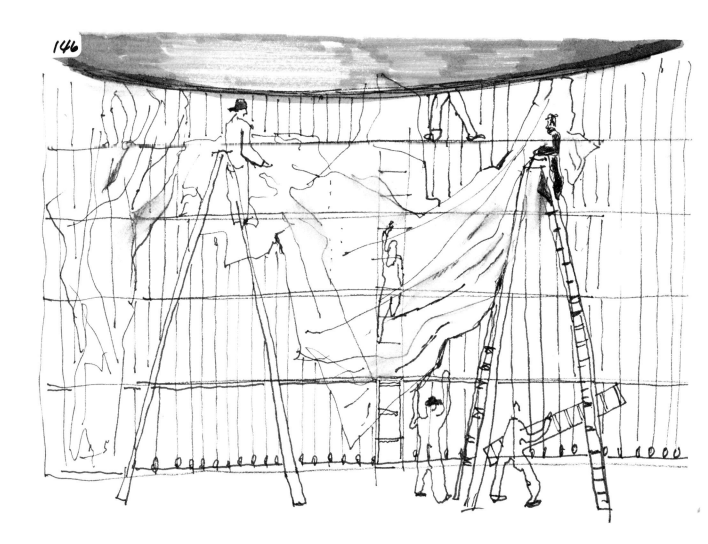

Stockholm-Stadsteatern
Parades & changes

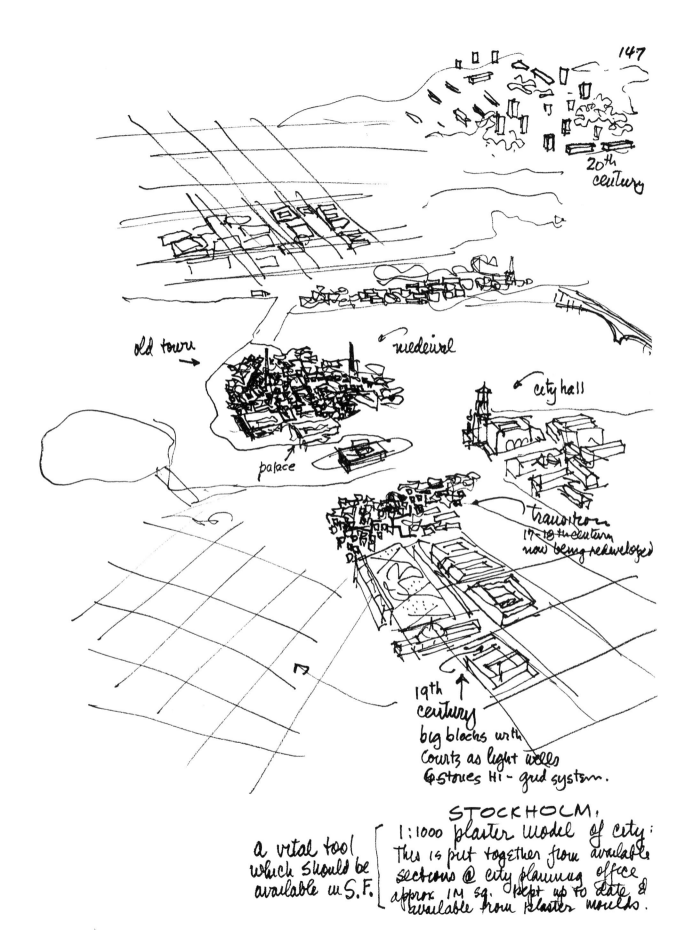

20th century

old town →

medieval

city hall

palace

transition
17-18th century
now being redeveloped

19th
century
big blocks with
Courts as light wells
6 stories Hi - grid system.

a vital tool
which should be
available in S.F.

STOCKHOLM,
1:1000 plaster Model of city:
This is put together from available
sections @ city planning office
approx 1M sq. kept up to date &
available from plaster moulds.

TAPIÖLA "Garden city"
from restaurant on
13th floor Hi rise
at town centrum
Mon Sept. 13

Notes on Tapiola

1. The architecture as such is <u>much</u> better than any of the Swedish new Town things. Not sure why.

2. <u>All</u> buildings are <u>white</u> which gives a wonderful unified quality throughout the whole scheme -- (some of the private houses are dark wood & brick) The white is of much different materials - brick. cemesto, ~~~~ galvanized iron, concrete - precast conc etc.

3. The Hi Rise not as high as the Vallingby Farsta. particularly Farsta - These are mostly 7-9 with the office block @ 13 . Scale is better.

4. The mixture of dwelling types is very large & much more interesting

5. Arrival & the formal center quality is excellent

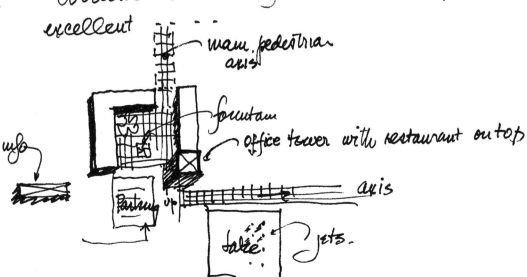

Ch-ch-ch
ch-ch

boil up from
under

waves

clich
clich

surface

Whoosh

over rocks

Swirl

tip-tip
tip-tip

recede from shore

types of water movement - Sea Ranch

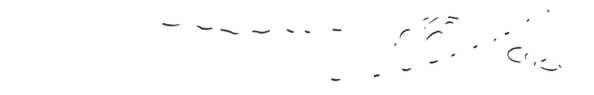

oct 26.   Sea Ranch
driftwood beach

Comments to myself on
visiting NorthPark Shopping Center, Dallas

As I think back many of the early ideas were right --- red brick throughout & particularly the shape of the walls

And more importantly the barrel vaults of red brick which led from plaza to mall to plaza these would have served to break down the endless corridors to manageable scale

our early fears that this would look inevitably like an airport has unfortunately happened. I am sad !!! The whole thing seems meaningless & slick and dull with no real life to its spaces or sculpture to its forms.

It should of course be said that I was there on a dull rainy day - & what's more it was crowded with thousands of ladies busily enjoying being there.

MT. Tam from
Phoenix Lake
Nov 27-65

Forest Floor -
Nov 27 - 1965

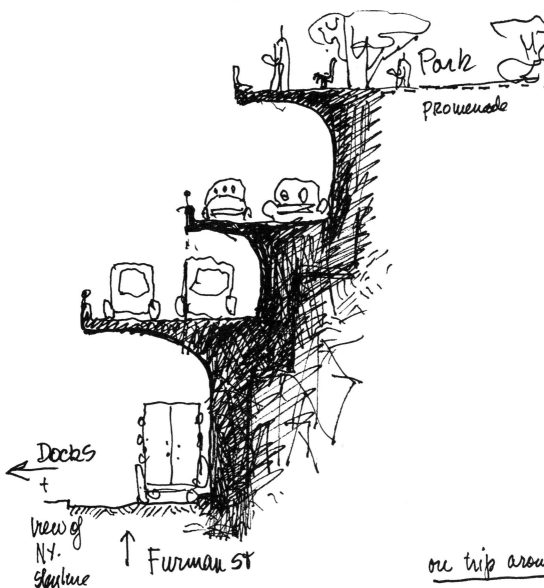

Park

PROMENADE

to Local street

Docks +

view of N.Y. Skyline

↑ Furman St

on trip around N.Y

Columbia heights.
Mike Rapuano consult.

one of the great examples of condensation
+ integration + amenity production of a
Highway in a city.

March 10, 1966

TO Highway
Consultants group [1]

Dear all —

On the way home at 30,000 feet &
after several american airlines martinni's I
am moved to thank you all for your creative
company in the past few days & also to say
again what I think is really wrong with highway
planning in the U.S.

I think our idea of doing a book is RIGHT

I also think we should, in order to make
our deliberations and decisions effective bring along
Alf Johnson & Joe Barnett & whoever else in
this vineyard needs to feel "part of the team"

But goddammit the real trouble with Highway
design in our country is that it has been given
over to a whole group of incompetent narrow
gauge, limited, unknowing, inept people who are
unable to deal or even understand the difficult
sophisticated and complex problem. Each one of us
at our our professional level would recoil in
horror if we had to deal with these kinds of
minds —— Structurally they are babies,
urban design-wise they dont have the foggiest

notion of what we're talking about—on an aesthetic level they are boors on a planning level they don't even comprehend the problem.

The issue as I see it really is that Highway designers are inadequately trained unfortunately selected and poorly educated. Also they are people with limited outlooks, and boors, if you wish, in a cultural sense. who are entrusted with the most difficult and sophisticated problems of our times. This is the <u>real</u> problem.

what we need to do, I think, is educate new young broad guage people who can <u>really</u> cope with this problem.

I would welcome your comments

L.

⇨ In rereading this the next day I propose to make it more positive by setting up educational proceedures for highway designers which cover such germane subjects as urban design (town planning) sociology etc. architecture. in addition to their normal courses of study.

Notes For the Summer Workshop.

The apparent difference between modern? Theatre and the environment is not in fact extant. ------

An environment is in fact simply a theatre for action & interaction to occur. The physical features may be programmed but the activities – except on a specific level (tennis webbe etc.) – are not.
The real interaction is like a "happening" in that the events & their sequences are non-programmed but occur as a results of the constraints imposed by the environment.

One can take the theatre as a mirror image of environmental design in that the classical theatre has a programmatic structure of events – vocal etc which occur on a sequenced basis ie: a play. & thus the environment is affected.
The ordinary planned environment is planned and designed on a sequenced or organized basis which affects what happens within it. But if the environment is permissive and non programmed then the events could be (or what people do! in) & vice versa.
This interrelation between fixed environment and fixed or non-fixed events – both ways – is one of the major things we wish to look into.......

trunk of Ceanothus
Mar '20

Thots for myself **

1. Wrong people living at the right densities :- poor should be at low - rich @ high

2. Also relation to downtown is reversed. rich should live close to downtown

3. we need a series of freedoms:

freedom from:	asphalt	want	brick - cobbles - granite
"	cars	"	pedes. precincts
"	sound	"	birds or music (as in Piazza San Marco)
" Endless	grid	"	interesting vistas
"	rush	"	sidewalk cafés
"	drabness	"	color, fountains
need for weekend escape		"	city which entices one to stay in town on weekend
mercury vapor		-	fine light standards for pedes
foot weariness		-	benches & places to sit.
architectural tooth pulling		-	streets which have facades.
amorphous quality		-	form which is understandable
hamburger joints		-	elegant restaurants
physical irritants		-	ecologically sound environment
desecration of natural features		-	waterfront promenade hilltop views
reliance on car		-	fine transportation & very varied
one kind of city		-	multiplicity
suburb		-	new towns

freedom   __want__

unilateral approach to transport - integrated both planning it & bldg it....

present day city   -   regional city which includes regional recreation - green belts - conservation - parks

conception of culture as market place   -   culture as a process of involvement for all citizens.

conception of city as an object   -   city as a great activity

idea that environment makes people happy

162

Experiments in
environment

Sea Ranch.
MONDAY
July 4th
Workshop problem with
Chuck Moore.
at Driftwood
beach

Nancy & Bill's –
an intimate warm "home"

➡ Build a city out of driftwood – with structures
you could live in – all related to each other –
Total area available – 50 yds across – from the
cliff to the ocean

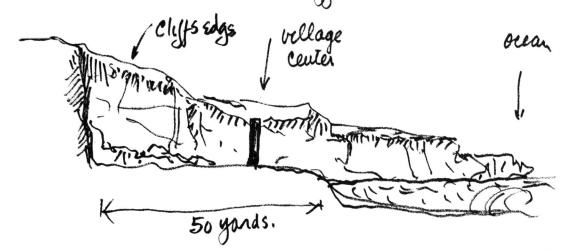

Cliffs edge

village
Center

ocean

50 yards.

Ann Halbecks
+ Steve & Bob
a site for rituals

A structure at the edge of the sea —
a viewing platform. attached to the land
but oriented to the ocean. the platform is
static but the sea swirls up under it —
Jim Huel - Lori Grunberg

Norma - A place to lie down in &
sit in

Daria -

a place at the foot of the
cliff with a view & _axis_ to the sea.

Peter - A place up high on the cliff looking out to
the sea over the city.

Jim Jensen -

another small one 180' away

A sheltered area from the wind looking
out to sea in a prominent upper plateau - the
small repeat relates to it & _controls_ the whole
area between.

Don & Merrill

A gate with one
dug in actual space & an implied space outside ......

What emerges from this is how personalized the structures people build are if left to their own devices & where public opinion (and resale value) are not a factor -- the direct response gives enormous insight into the person's interior desires and personality -- his interests and attitudes.

The driftwood itself is an ExcellEnt material to work with because it has its own inherent sculptural qualities it is fairly light weight and is immediately Evocative - without doing anything particular to it - - - - the very choice of shape makes incredible events possible.

The same problem could be given with BOXES (as with Joan Yost's project with the children) & it would be different -- we should try that also on a succeeding project sometime to explore the difference in results due to material...

→ Also by using driftwood (only) the whole scheme automatically achieves an inherent unity — as in old villages.....

PATH problem
wed afternoon

The path as an idea:

1- as a connector between points ie: home → work, work → shopping etc.

2- The path as a release:
Hiking for pleasure
walking

3- The path as exercise:
H.T. walking etc.

4. The path as an experience for the senses- see, hear, smell
KINESTHETICS
at which point it tends to transfer to

5- The path as a series of events, happenings, interractions etc.

This could be a way to order
the paths - all cross the main artery path

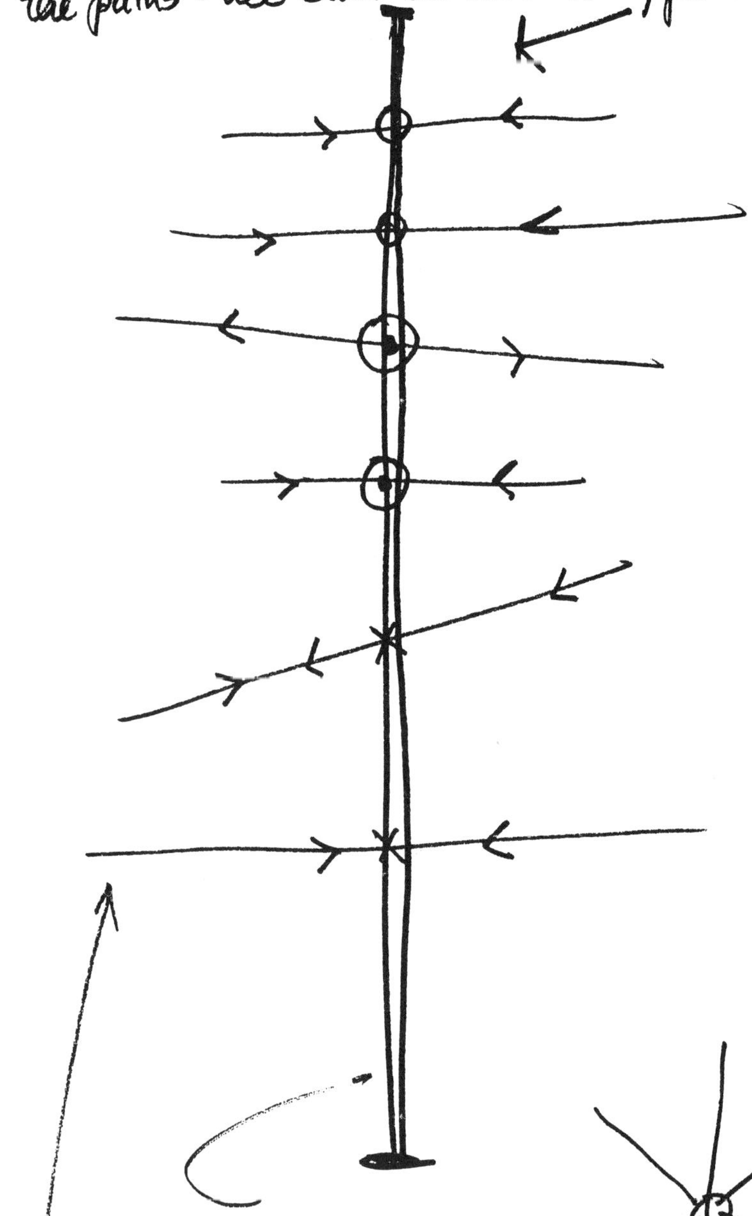

Forms for the paths problem

medieval
structure
w/walls

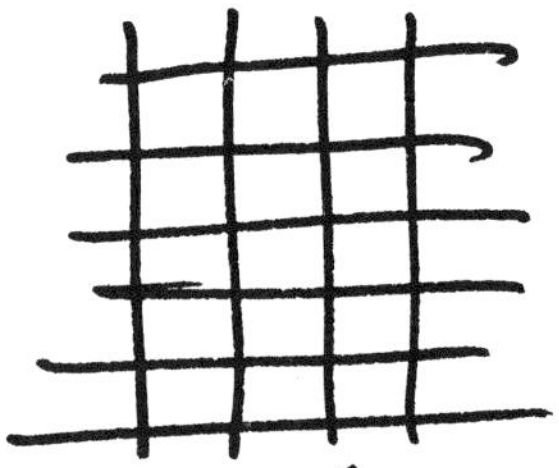

american 19th
cent grid

20th century
freeway loop

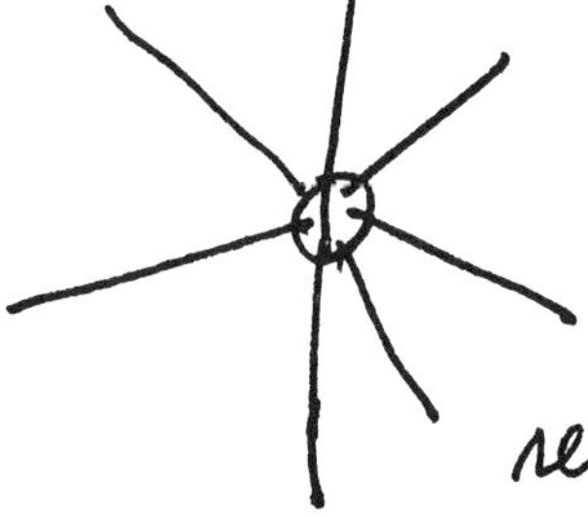

main spine to
be ordered

Side paths intersect &
non-ordered by individual

renaissance rond-pont

possible form for a regional or
megalopitan - transportation network

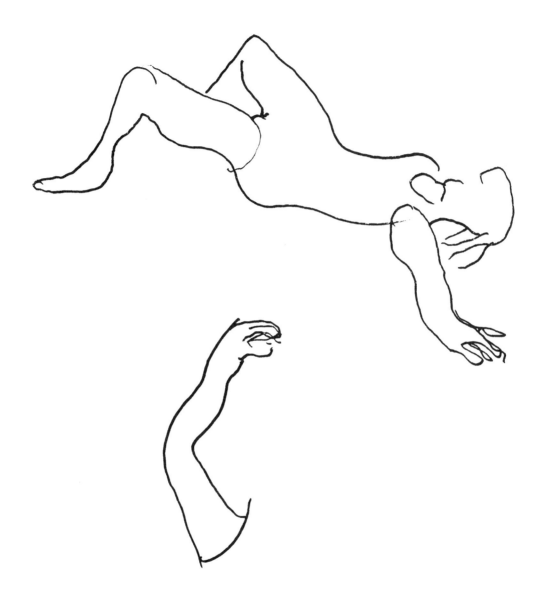

Start with floor
& own body

move body on
floor noticing space
between body & floor

start relating space
to other people

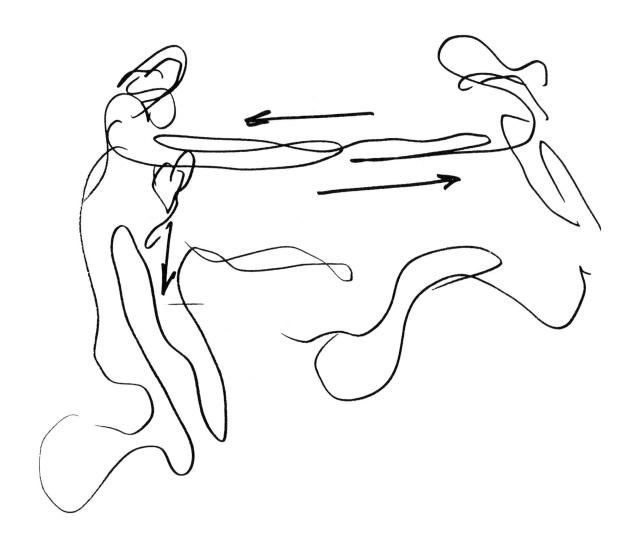

start working with
other people.

feel the floor under your body

174

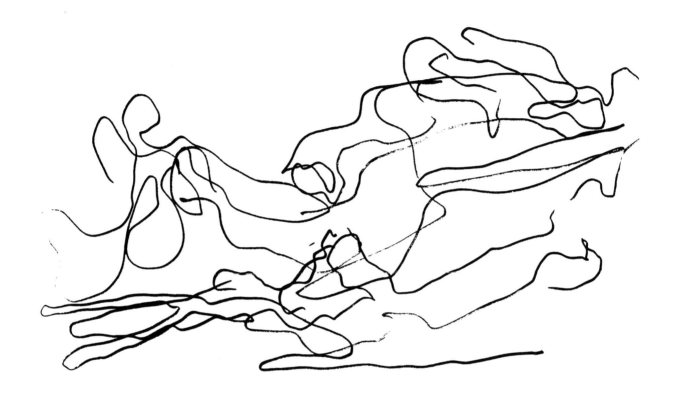

Start growing over
to walls

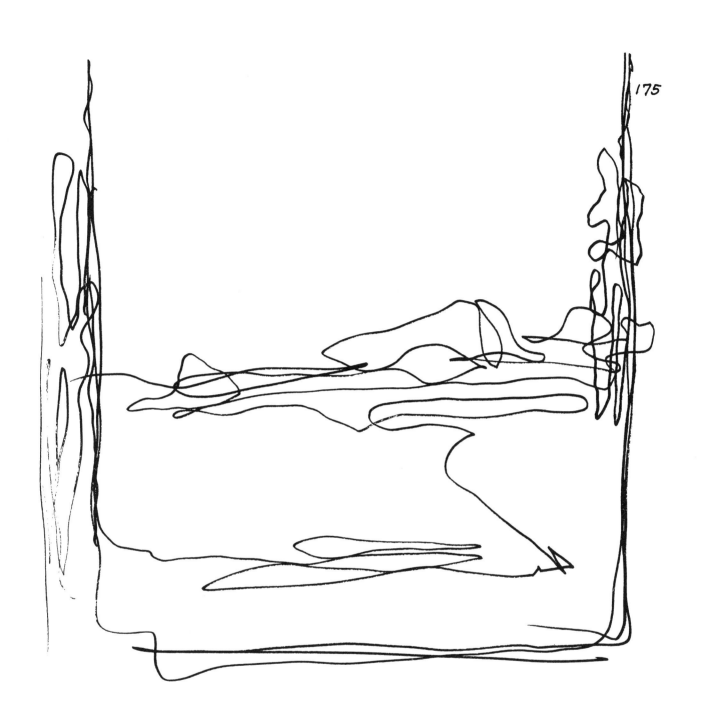

175

work with the
space between walls

wallo

when spaces become focus of movement this
will establish the group configurations & composition
automatically — the artist of time well establish
the shape & rhythms of configurations

| NOTE | - The restrictions
create the form ...
Like in <u>nature</u> -- sandstone
erodes more quickly than
granite ∴ the granite stays as
perceivable round balls.
or in the driftwood city --
the driftwood shapes created
the forms of the structures..
In this dance problem - the space
focus ie: wall - floor - space -
between - people, will create the
configurations .

JIM S - Do you mean <u>we</u> are like the driftwood
N<u>o</u>- In the dance you are both the
material & the former or builder.

180

usual
waterfall
as @ Portland
(starts at top)

50'-80'

↑ Bowl
┬ water plane

idea for a fountain .... concrete planes
in many dimensions connected by steps
water seeping into bowl from surging
mass on all sides — from below not
top.

↑ new bench

Lovejoy - Portland
sculpture

In the plaza there should be events.... sculpture
shows - concerts - dance events with dancers all
over AND arriving to center space from above
down stairs around fountain...
Pots of geraniums ok .- locate these - check design &
send to Kenward.

182

Halprin
Sea Ranch aug 2.

Alhambra
aug '66

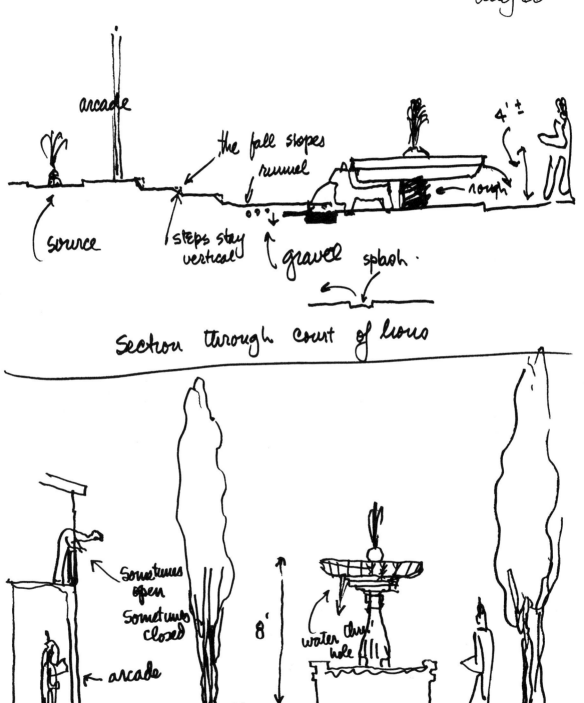

arcade

the fall slopes
runnel

4' ±

rough

source

steps stay
vertical

gravel

splash

Section through court of lions

Sometimes
open
Sometimes
closed

arcade

8'

water thru'
hole

Seville —
court of oranges
at Cathedral

irrigation
Channels
one brick wide

These lead to each tree but from various main
Channels... source of water is the fountain & jet.
at intervals a brick goes across channel (with a hole
thru' (like a tiny bridge) which gives a kind of dot dash
quality to the whole floor

Notes on Climate control in Spain :—

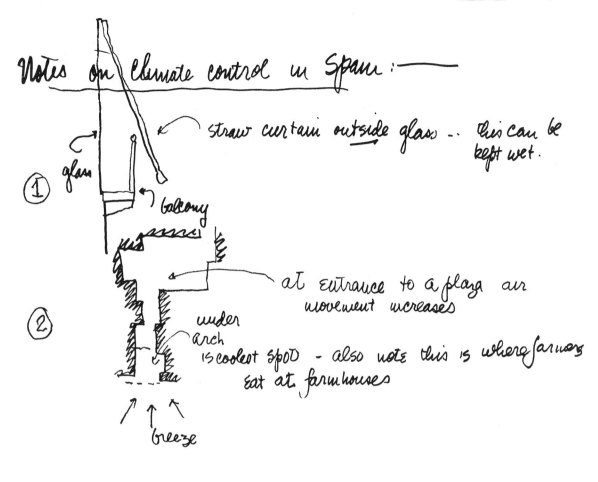

straw curtain outside glass .. this can be kept wet.

① glass

balcony

at entrance to a plaza air movement increases

② under arch is coolest spot - also note this is where farmers eat at farmhouses

breeze

③ at turns in direction air movement increases

④ in narrow alleys sun does not penetrate & is ∴ cool

⑤ courts act as ventilators

⑥

breezes

Same principle in small plazas - act as wind vents.

⑦

↑ air movement

balconies & bay windows
catch air movement.

Points To Be checked on site

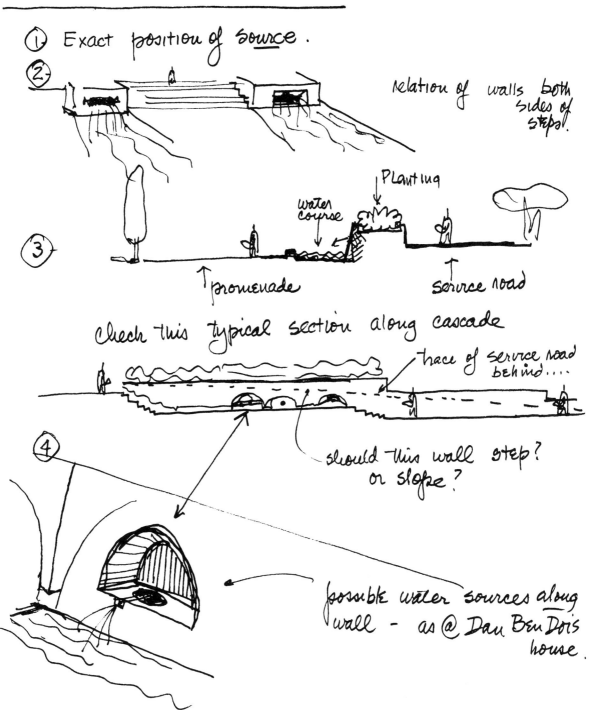

① Exact position of source.

②

relation of walls both sides of steps.

③

Planting

water course

↑ promenade

↑ service road

Check this typical section along cascade

trace of service road behind....

④

should this wall step? or slope?

possible water sources along wall - as @ Dan Ben Dois house.

Masada –
Sept 1st

190

Embarcadero Plaza
& Fountain ....
    Program notes to be given
    to the sculptors participating
    in the competition ....

                Saturday Dec 3 - 1966

STATEMENT TO SCULPTORS

This work has been conceived of as a total
environment in which all the elements
working together create an place for
participation. The Locus is the termination
of Market Street - major boulevard in
the city - the Embarcadero freeway
encloses the space on the East in
massive and dramatic concrete & includes the
movement of cars. There will be an enormous
building complex to the West with
terraces, platforms shops restaurants
focusing down to the plaza. Many people.
        The plaza is a theatre for
events to happen.

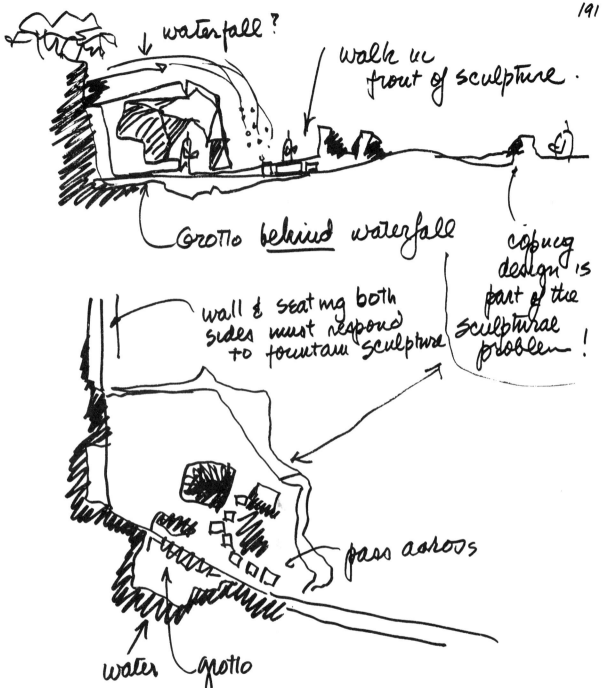

waterfall ?

walk in front of sculpture.

Grotto behind waterfall

coping design is part of the sculptural problem !

wall & seating both sides must respond to fountain sculpture

pass across

water   grotto

The fountain is the pivotal
point in the plaza.

It has been purposely placed
off the axis of Market Street to
avoid the Renaissance quality of
objects in visual static relationship &
to one point perspective.

The back wall defines the space.
It also serves as wind and sun
trap.

The <u>sculpture</u> is an outgrowth of
the wall and not thought of
as a separate element in space

It is an environmental event
in which water, light & people
are as much a part of the
sculpture as are the solid
forms.

It is basically made of
concrete because it must be

part of the environment NOT
an object within it ....

→ 9- We should help the sculptors (particularly
the foreign ones) by giving some `rule of thumb`
cost for concrete per yard so as to give
them some indications of what is achievable.

10- Height (maximum) of the back wall
must be established by us.
we should prepare a section!

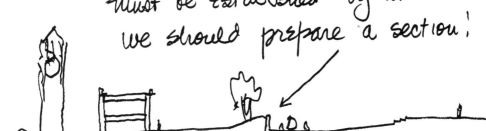

THE SCULPTORS

MASON	-	L.A.
MELCHERT	-	Berkeley
NAKIAN	-	New York
OVERHOFF	-	S.F.
PENALBA	-	Paris
VAILLANCOURT	-	Canada

<u>Fred Simpich</u>
cc Al Boeke

Jan 3, 1967

Dear Fred:—

The recent Governor's award program premiated the Sea Ranch more than any other project in the State. As you may perhaps know it received the highest award possible for Master Planning — the award for exceptional distinction. In addition it received awards for the houses (Esherick) the Store (Esherick) the condominiums (Moore) the graphics (Stauffacher)

I am pleased of course, as I know you must be. But that is not the point of this letter. I have been up at the ranch during Xmas & while I was there I kept thinking of what the Sea Ranch has come to mean to many people. It has become a symbol of an attitude and an approach. The attitude is that quality is worthwhile in itself but that it also makes great economic sense. The approach is that it is possible for human beings to occupy & live in a piece of land without destroying the very values which brought them there in the first place.

The Sea Ranch has become a symbol for conservationists everywhere of the potential of living <u>with</u> the land rather than against it. When I say everywhere I mean just that. I am not sure you realize how widely the Ranch is known, particularly in professional circles, throughout the world for what it has come to stand for. Here, in this country, Secretary Udall is vitally interested, all levels of gov't. people are. They are interested, as are most architects, planners, landscape architects, conservationists because the S/R is a symbol of the private rather than the public sector dealing with land on a sensitive level. They believe what we have been telling them that we are doing and stand for. *

It would be a terrible blow if all this were to change. I can't tell you how many high hopes would be dashed, how many ideals would be broken, how many important people would be disillusioned; quite aside from those of us to whom the Sea Ranch means so much personally.

I write all this because I get rumors of all kinds which imply disenchantment, high pressure sales tactics, changes in policy, modifications to basic planning. In fact, as you know, neither I nor any of my colleagues seem any longer to be involved in any planning. ~~Not as I understand it~~ & I have been informed that neither are Al Boeke or Jeff Fairfax.. who is?

what can I do? what can I, or any of us, do to prevent a drift which seems to be taking place.

Best regards & a ~~Happy~~ New Year

Larry

196

Waterfalls at
Phoenix Lake.
Sun - Jan 29-67

I used to believe that the root cause of uglification in America lay with the American people. And that the reason for ~~the~~ despoilation of our countryside, the poor quality of our urban architecture, the billboards hiding our scenic resources, the junk yards, the smog, the noise, the dust, the traffic jams, the violation of our natural resources, the incredible mess our curlization has made of its environment was all our fault as a culture. I believed that other, more ancient curlizations had found the way back to Eden and because of their greater share of artistic sensibilities had discovered how to build beautiful cities; preserve their countrysides, avoid blight enjoy good food and the good life......

There seemed considerable evidence to support the NOTION that America was being ruined by Americans whereas Europe was being delightfully preserved by Europeans. The Evidence was there on all sides - Paris, Rome, Amsterdam, Budapest, the Alps, Portofino, the old city of Jerusalem the Adriatic coast, Mykonos the hill towns of Italy Each was a delight ... city and countryside had achieved a kind of incredibly happy balance where each enhanced the other the countryside was romantic and beautiful the cities varied, interesting and exciting - an adventure.

In America where man goes ugliness goes with him ... Instead of Paris we have produced Los Angeles instead of the Alps there is the South shore of Tahoe instead of Portofino we have Pacifica, instead of the coliseum in Rome there is the parking lot around Candlestick Park. Instead of the via appia we have the Embarcadero Freeway. What is wrong with the American people and especially Californians that they have defiled the nest in which they live destroying the very qualities of environment which make it the Golden State of the Nation. MEA CULPA.

Recently I have gone back to Europe frequently and I am appalled by what I see! The new outskirts of Paris are a mess - the housing developments outside Rome are as bad as Stuyvesant town in New York and that's pretty bad. London is invaded by he rise unpleasant skyscrapers and recently while I was in Jerusalem I engaged in a battle to preserve an ancient, beautiful, monument dating back to the crusades from destruction by a freeway. The Seine is also being cut off from Paris by a freeway.

They am less sure now than I was before that other people and other places have found 'answers' through sensitivities which we lack don't have to the searing problems of our time. As I dig more deeply I am less convinced than I was that there is a carryover from the great abilities of the medieval church builders to the problems of our own day. or that the Renaissance lessons of the lessons help Europe in the way they should. European results when faced by population explosion the onslaught of the automobile, 2 cars in every garage, television, the affluent society seem no better than our own.

PRINCIPLES

1- When there is a conflict between resident & auto driver — the resident should be favored.

2- Prefer _not_ to disrupt existing neighborhood.

3- Where disruption proves imperative bring in design concept group to establish principles . . . .

4- ABSorptive capacity of cars in a city — must be determined and then the #s of cars limited to that #

5- Highways should not be built where they obliterate possibilities for future improvement ie: New Orleans opening up waterfront

6- Important civic values should not be destroyed by freeways ie: vieux carré.

7. The environment is as much a concern of Hway designers as moving traffic —

8. ALL Highway designers should have training in the following disciplines:
Landscape architecture
architecture
urban design
Planning

(NOTE: ① distribute principles in advance of next mtg. which is in TOM KAVANAUGH'S office
② send letter to TOM K. re: staff costs @ lump sum for "values procedure" with short description of what we are planning to do)

<u>Function</u> - does it <u>work</u> for the users -

<u>Relatedness</u> - is it in good relation to the rest of its environment - -

ie: dirt is only something out of place : ugliness is something in the wrong place..... signs etc.

<u>Integrity</u> - does it have its own inherent qualities or is it being used to "improve" something else.

<u>Involvement</u>. does it involve people in their own creativity - Chalk Fillmore

<u>Current needs</u>. Needs change & ∴ we must plug in opportunities for change.

:. apply to age groups

Young people - gathering dancing Tivoli

drumming competitions drag racing. ·

Human Be-ins

<u>USE OF Natural resources</u>

waterfronts views. pollution

NEW ORLEANS
Analysis on site of
vieux carré etc

april 12 1967

JAX

from ferry.

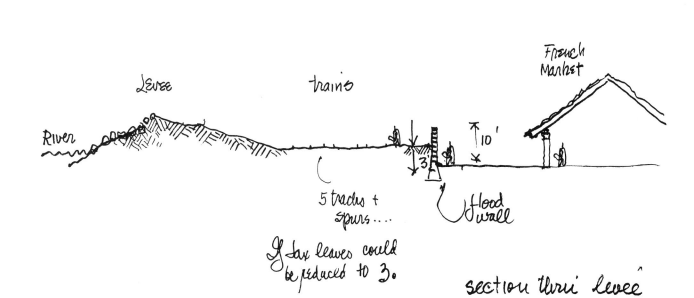

River

Levee

trains

French
Market

5 tracks +
spurs....

If Jax leaves could
be reduced to 3.

10'

3'

Flood
wall

section thru levee

HALPRIN STATEMENT to
LOWELL BRIDWELL - BPR -
on NEW ORLEANS FREEWAY

Diffidence in coming in from outside.

Gradually have felt that the importance
outweighed the local importance of ^majority. home rule.

Went down with Experience of S.F - which was
not integrated with anything —
Mayor said this is "his first honest
mistake"

② Studies of freeways throughout world.

Did not start with bias against elevated
Hways or for that matter against
freeways along waterfronts. Many structures
as such are extremely handsome....
There are good examples of both ! Have
so stated in my book & in many speeches.
Where these occur they have been
sensitive examples of integrated
planning.

I felt after looking at the situation
that the elevated freeway ^as planned would
in fact hurt the Vieux Carré,
plus Jackson Square & also
the whole incredible resource of
the New Orleans waterfront

I must be frank in saying I hoped that an 205
obviously good solution would come to me - it did not!

I fear a destruction of the qualities
of the environment & a blighting--
including the removal of future possibilities-
→ question of quantification systems

→ I cannot agree personally with the view
that we cannot stop the world while
we make up our minds. Especially
when we all are convinced that
the impact will be deleterious Stop
it until a satisfactory solution is reached.

The tide has changed.

There is a new spirit afoot.

The White House conference on Natural
Beauty, the Highway Beautification
act the HUD Demonstration Cities
grants are all demonstrations

The word beauty has changed
from an insult to a description of
what we want!

There is a National Council on the Arts
  "   "   "   Advisory Comm " Hist. Sites
  "   "   " city called S.F. which turned
    down freeway
  "   "   constant letters for better fways
    throughout country
Your own attitudes have changed radically.

Do not throw
the baby out with
the bath water-
commun. value of
transport. must be
subs to the city
otherwise us pt. to 17

There is increasing awareness of the
impact of all elements of the environment.

The fact is that many people do <u>not</u> become
aware of the impact of a feature until after
it is done - viz S.F.

In my view there are several options

1- Restudy this route on an
integrated basis with freeway as
part of the total development.

2. Study <u>all</u> alternative routes.
reaching for other ways

→ 3. Do NOT Build -
this would have to develop from
facts . not be a bias .

I urge you to send down an able,
highly creative concept group -
Certainly with your support
Possibly backed by other agencies
Hopefully by the mayor etc

To work on a crash program to
explore ideas. Back it up with
a major analysis of the whole city plan

It should be made up of professionals
of the highest order of competence.
      Planners - urban designers.
      Architects   etc. etc.
      Lands. Arch.
      Structural engineers

It is too bad that there is a feeling
that designers are vs engineers. What
is being asked for is competence & training
in the field of environment - the problem
is also one of study techniques - the use
of 3 dimensional attitudes etc.

There seems to constantly crop up the
feeling that just because bad things
have been done we should condone
more...... PHOO to that - I don't
even think anyone believes it...

208

people
within landscape

people
vs landscape

PAST ⟹ EXISTING ⟷ TECHNIQUES

GOALS
- WHAT
- HOW
- CONFLICTS
* - INTERRELATIONS *

art process
1- linear attach on goal - Renaissance
2- Multifacetted complex recognition of change as part of techn.
multi media

Education: for complexity . NOT SIMPLICITY .
" change
not alternatives between 2 things but complex interweaving - influence of each thing on the other : computerized techniques as tools for disclosing possibilities . also to disclose implications of actions :⟷
HOW 1 action affects another .
.... art = science ....

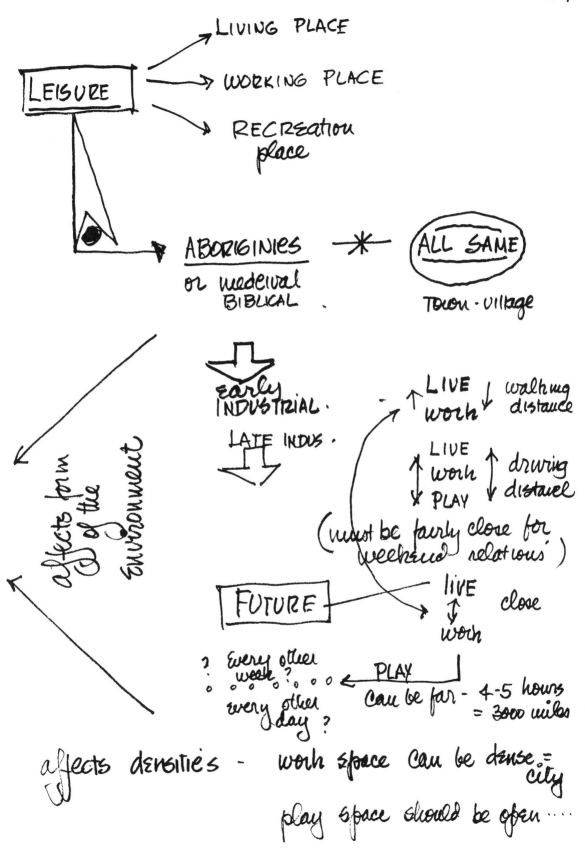

LIVING PLACE

LEISURE → WORKING PLACE

→ RECREATION place

ABORIGINIES ✳ (ALL SAME)
or medeival
BIBLICAL . TOWN · village

early
INDUSTRIAL.

LATE INDUS.

affects form of the environment

↑ LIVE / work ↓ walking distance

LIVE / ↑work↑ / ↓PLAY↓ driving distance

(must be fairly close for weekend relations)

FUTURE → live ↕ work close

? Every other week ? ← PLAY Can be far - 4-5 hours = 3000 miles
every other day ?

affects densities - work space can be dense.= city

play space should be open .....

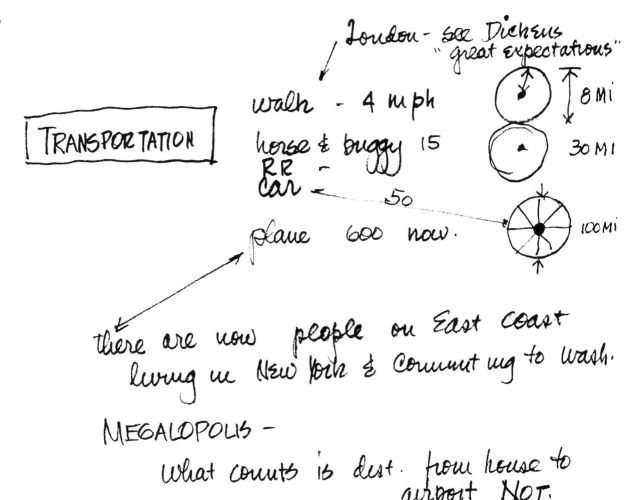

London - see Dickens
"great expectations"

TRANSPORTATION

walk - 4 mph   8 Mi

horse & buggy 15   30 Mi
RR -
car -   50

plane 600 now.   100 Mi

there are now people on East coast
living in New York & Commuting to Wash.

MEGALOPOLIS -

What counts is dist. from house to
airport NOT.
house ⟶ work.

NOTE   ecosystems - complex interactions
over period of change

DISCLIMAX → CONDITION = stability ↱ environmental
                              instability ↲ stability
                         change ← caused by fire, Earthq

| Human dynamics |

change is constant ↕ ↕ of
⇧ ⇧ control of environment
+ rapid inventions

In earlier times - people were in a constant period
of climax - major modifying influences was
war

Now we are entering into a continuous
period of DISCLIMAX ↕ of rapidity of
inventions

| CHANGES IN SIZE ⫸   hardware gets smaller
                         (Super Heterodyne
                          radio vs. Trans)
                       No's get larger = envelopes.

GOALS ←——→ HARDWARE

PROCESSES

This is a closed system ······

   <u>Goals</u> will be modified by both hardware
        and processes

<u>Hardware</u> - incredibly varied over time

<u>processes</u> this has some constancy ····

(A) new para...

The recovery of the cut-over slopes will go through various phases of course. They need to reestablish a new ecology... a series of new community relations... new plant groupings will occur. NOT the old stand of pure redwoods. On many cut-over lands particularly in the RELIM company we saw much alder ~~and~~ coming up ... in many areas the douglas fir percentage is greater – after all the redwood forest is a climax condition and cannot re-establish itself over night. The letting in of light and air encourages some species and discourages others.

At all events the first years after cutting will serve to hold ones breath and wait for the bombed out aspect to simply clothe over. After about 20 years that will have happened and then after approximately another 30 a new forest will have appeared. By then perhaps these 2nd growth areas will have achieved enough stature (as they have, for example, on the logged over areas of Mendocino & Northern Sonoma county in Sea Ranch) as to make camp grounds feasible amongst ✓ the 2 growth timber

Ⓑ At this moment it is very difficult to adequately cruise and understand the Redwood Creek area. Only those ~~parts~~ which have been logged or are being readied for logging are accessible by road. This puts this area at a distinct disadvantage on an evaluative level when compared to Mill Creek which has been handsomely prepared for visitors over the years as part of the state Park system. We flew it, of course, but that is no way to see and experience a forest -- it is more like looking at a photo mosaic. The qualities of scale & environment & "feel" & smell which we discussed at length — the sensory and emotional impact are not perceivable from the air — they must be dealt with on the ground.

Finally some comment is needed on the future development of the entire region and the need to PLAN the whole region for the future. The area is depressed - I believe it has the lowest per capita income in the State. It has been subjected to floods, tidal wave destruction and diminishing returns from its single economic base - lumbering.

REDWOOD LOGGING
practice

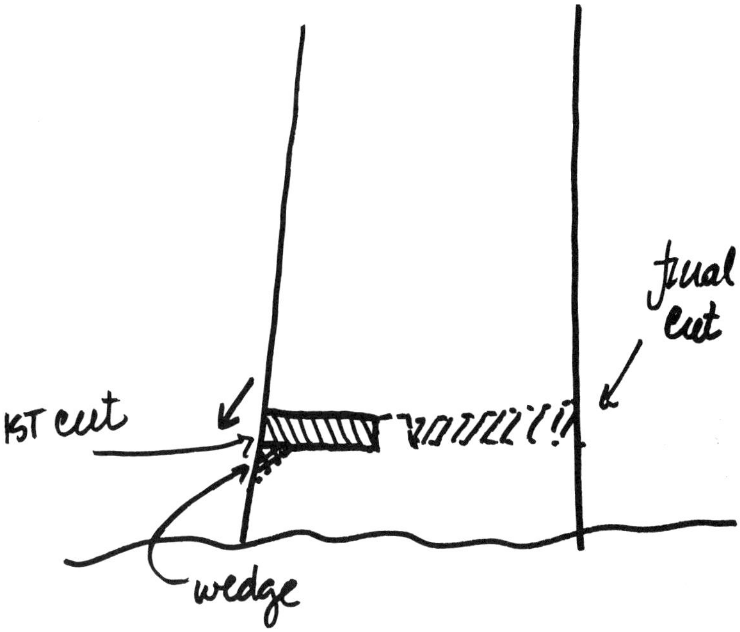

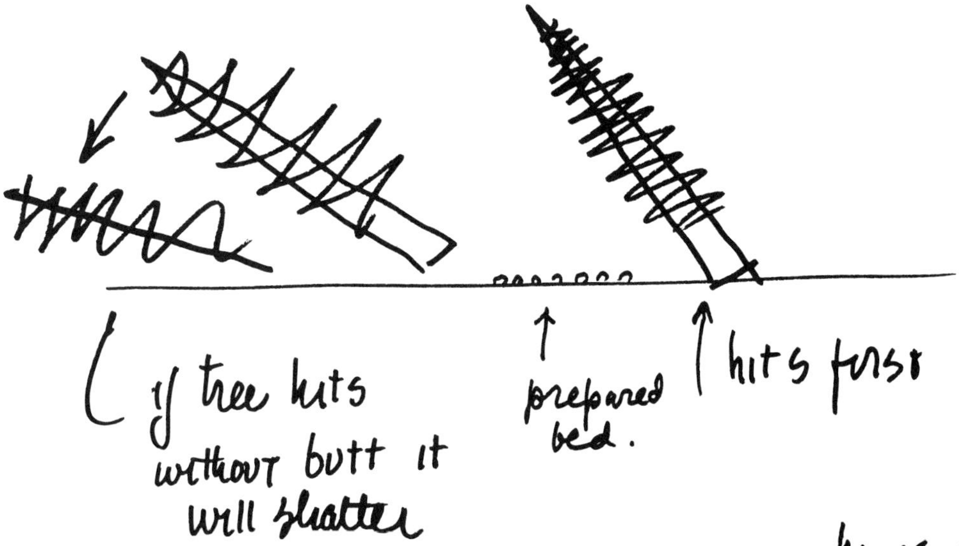

1st cut

final cut

hinge

wedge

if tree hits
without butt it
will shatter

↑
prepared
bed.

↑ hits first

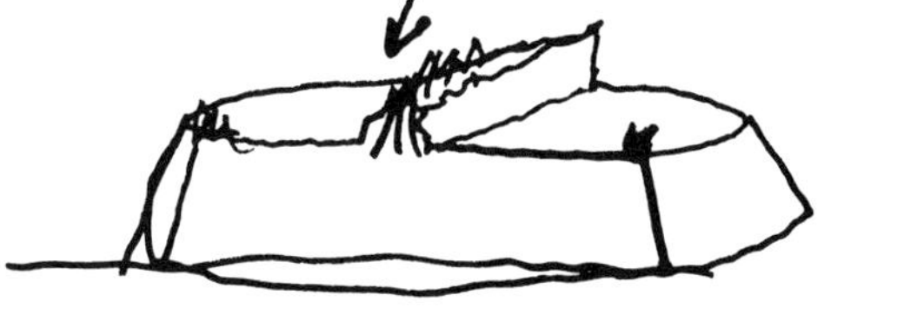

hinge at end

The diversification brought in by the National Park should be extremely advantageous, over the long haul, to the entire economy of the region.... the influx of tourists, the length of stay at the Park, all will upgrade the economy

But there are hidden dangers as well. Since the area is depressed economically there seems, at the moment, little ability to invest in Hi-quality accomodations in the environs of the Park. Nothing that has been built to date gives any indication of real quality for the future. We heard complaints from Redwood Company representatives that no tourists are now coming — yet when we spoke of the need to invest capital in improvements to draw them & keep them there — (restaurants, good motels etc) we drew a complete blank.

There is a real danger that the area could develop into a National Park Slum if ad-hoc, cheap, improvements are started based on inadequate capitalization and inadequate standards of regional planning & Control — private investment in the area must be of National Park standards as well as Park investment itself.

There is urgency for a comprehensive Regional Plan which will incorporate future development on Park Lands but even _more_ importantly establish criteria & controls for other facilities as well — the town center, the shopping facilities, private camping, motels, restaurants, theatres etc. _all_ need careful advance planning. I think it should be mandatory that the proposed freeway location & design be carefully integrated into the Park proposals — NOT vice versa. Building a freeway now without integrated planning would be a disaster!

What is needed is a careful overview of the environment of the Park — not only the Park itself. I think this is true anywhere It is particularly true here where the problems of economics and ability to develop are so great and the size of the Park is so ~~small~~ modest. Given an enormous acreage a Park can almost establish its own environment — its own buffers. Here this is not true — the external environment impinges on all sides and must be controlled for the sake of the Park.

ⓒ What we need, of course, is to get it all .. all the remaining timber in the area should be preserved — even then there would be little enough! If that is impossible then we should get as much as possible on New Land; not, I believe, simply consolidate and round out the corners of what is already in Public ownership and will be in any event preserved.

We need to hurry!!

But we should hurry in the right direction.

Engleman Fir
at MT. ararat

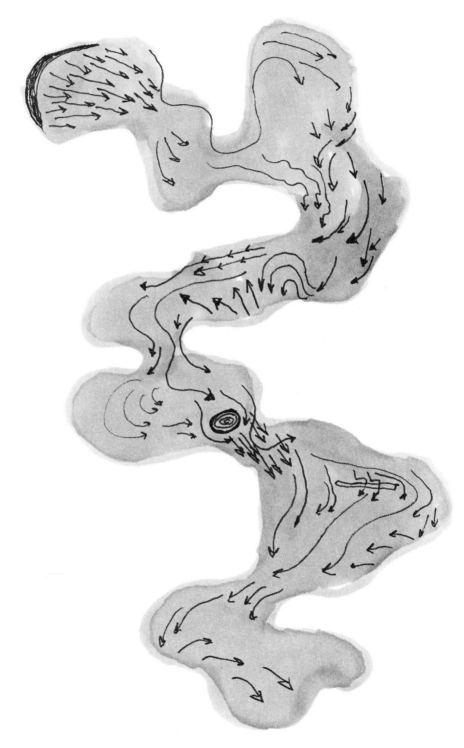

Stream.
Indian Hennego

water level

ice

Section

lake
bottom

ice forms in lake —
mirror lake —

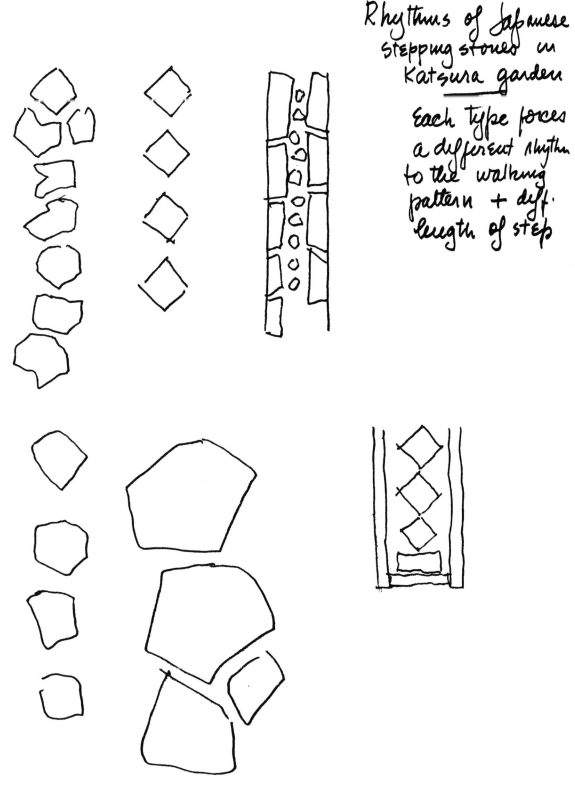

Rhythms of Japanese
stepping stones in
Katsura garden

Each type forces
a different rhythm
to the walking
pattern + diff.
length of step

Trip to Japan, for
work with Breuer & Tange on
Flushing meadows -- July 1967

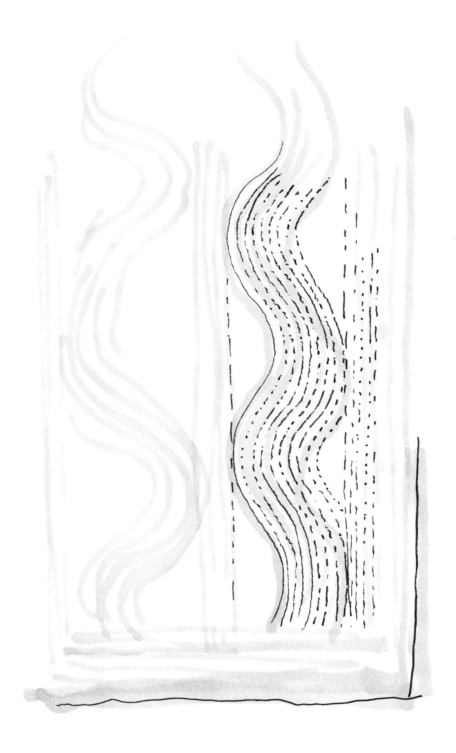

sand pattern
Nanzen-ji

SUMIYA INN
KYOTO

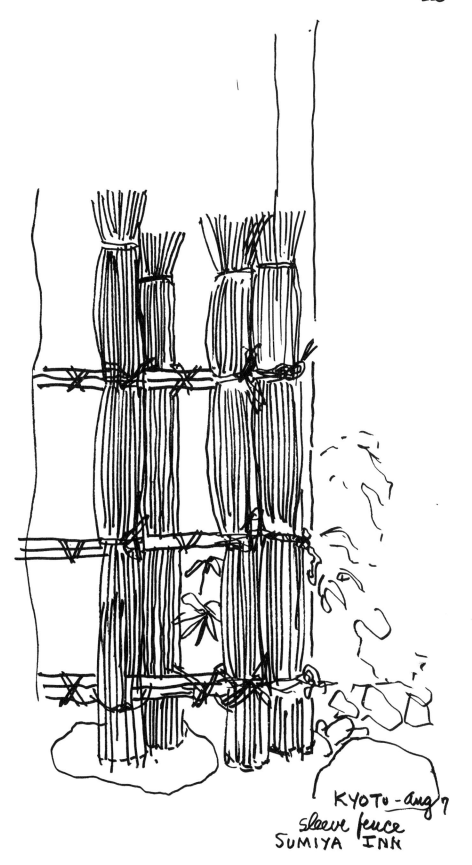

KYOTO - aug '7
sleeve fence
SUMIYA INN

→ NOTS. on the small Japanese garden

The horizontal pattern is very strong while the vertical is undifferentiated ie: walls & backgrounds are played down

water ← tan stucco - no pattern

← strong pattern

sleeve fence

This keeps the eye low & away from the confinement of background

The space also is always in motion - around objects & carried sideways by both the stone patterns AND the non-closure by sleeve fences

Lantern water stone

10'

Sleeve fence   12'

The enjoyment of the garden is always from floor level which is about 3' below our eye height - this puts everything in a completely different perspective...... much less planar.... (Rana says that everything is low for them becuz their eyes are horizontal ⬲ rather than Round 👁 like ours)

Scale is different ...

basin   MOUND   viewing platform
waterfall

NANZEN-JI - tea ceremony garden

You cannot see the base of the waterfall because of the mound.

228

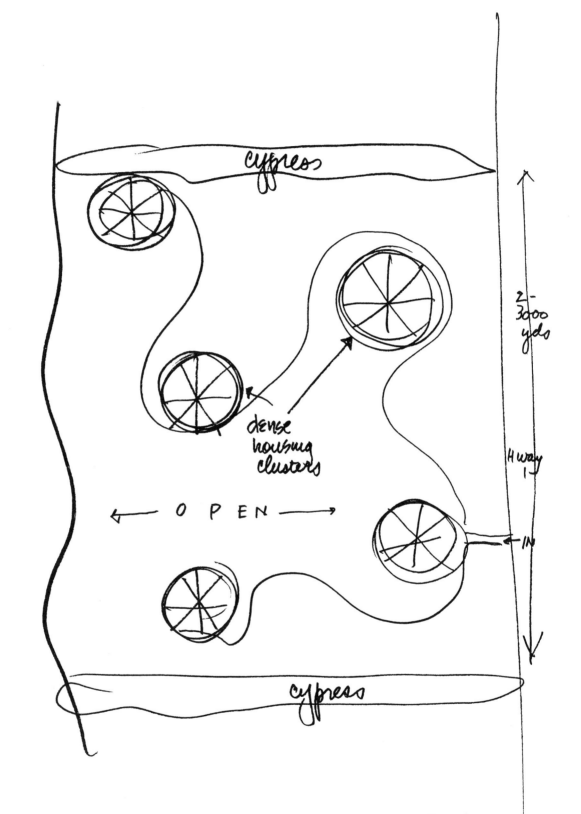

cypress

dense
housing
clusters

← O P E N →

cypress

2-
3000
yds

Hway
1

← IN

method of avoiding "subdivision"
look between long hedgerows.

Sea Ranch-
aug 27

Dear Wolf —

I am just back from Expo 67
at Montreal & wanted to let you
know my reactions. I was much moved
by it. And inspired in a strange way.
Not, I think, for the obvious reasons —
but because here all of a sudden one
can sense what the world's environment
could be like if we would only address
ourselves to the problem.

First of all the transportation is
superb. The car is left at the edge
of things and then the river, the islands,
the waterways are left free for enjoyment.
It is made possible of course by the
trains which take you from island to
island and then the delightful little
minirails which move about at different
levels at majestic speeds — not too
fast not too slowly supported by

light their columns, soaring over the pedestrians quietly. No light & air is blocked, no foul-smelling fumes result no noise, no clatter, no parking problem. It is such a lovely & dignified solution to moving people about - one wonders why it is taking us _so_ long to apply this lesson to our cities.

and then the movement through the US pavilion is so superb it brings a whole new dimension into the quality of the environment.

I also much liked the differentiation of pedestrian levels - the arrival at upper decks

and platforms from which long ramps & stairs brought you down & up to exhibits & other facilities. For the first time the 3 dimensional qualities of a variety of transportation techniques became vividly apparent ....

My next strong impression was HABITAT. I think this is one of the significant pieces of architecture of our time. What seems most important to me is not its aesthetics which I like very much but its potential as a technique to bring humanity & scale at high density back into the city. It offers an alternate to the high tower in a vast open space (so bad for families)

& the overcostly low row house on the ground. It offers a possibility for real "pus in urbe" which we have all been looking for. In addition of course the variety is endless & - in quantities - I would assume the cost could get quite low. What beautiful 3 dimensionals streets, villages, & towns could be made in this way—all the charm of Italian hilltowns in a modern context —

The American pavilion sent me! Bucky Fuller's dome especially at twilight with the lights coming on inside really sent me. I have been in other domes but here for the first time the qualities of the space & the sense of an architecture really came through. And the exhibit was I thought delightful— I ENJOYED it - I even felt it was poignant & profound.. I enjoyed the levels, the movement up and down through the various spaces & at the top level I expect I got as close to the moon as I ever will. I have always been somewhat appalled at the thought of domes trying to create enormous controlled environments but here I felt good about it — the people really came through an importance on the ~~right~~ inside.

In the long run though no <u>one</u> thing comes through as much to me as the totality of the environment — the dignity & fun of it all and the fact that it is all working for people to feel <u>good</u> in → Transport, buildings, open spaces a cacaphony of fine interrelations. Why cant we do this everywhere?

Best

Larry

234

discussion w/ PAUL BAUM
re: psychological effects
of the environment
Oct 25-'67

Self - images as a generator of what we think the environment ought to be.

basic uniformity ie: birth - family - love - these are universal

are environments important at all? to happiness to people's well being.....

WHAT ARE WE LOOKING FOR - A minimum platform of required amenities

Amenities :   in the environment which can be considered necessity

   Freedom from :   Noise -
                     air pollution -
                     autos ⟨ visual hazard
                     hazards............
                     filth ? = rats. (not neatness)
                        (psych att. towards shit)
                        ie: do we start with a
                        requirement for cleanliness
                        or is this a derived need.

varies with class → middle
                     lower
                     upper.

privacy is →   overcrowding. ie: physical
required for   @ sexual relations
                  (paul questions this)
                  Points out need public sexual intercourse

Note collectives --- KIBBUTZ ← → Change over time - showers.
   in the early days all usual criteria challenged - now very middle
   does this mean environments change? class.
   ie: the environmental needs of people are not static → either change
                                                            the environ.
                                                            OR
   where do young people screw?   Move to a
                                                            diff. environ.
   same as: place for young people to get together
            without supervision....

   Thus affects peoples memories of ↓ if it is   Early experience
experienced in basement then implies dank, dirty etc.
        to describe the experience ... is this why people
   consider sex dirty & secretive ?

comment: the crowding in subways is for most people extremely pleasant & has significant sexual overtones

(b) privacy ie: room for carrying on your own interests..

converse = isolation ie: loneliness.

Paul questions this whole overcrowding concept — major problem he thinks is isolation not feeling of privacy. the converse of this is solitary confinement !

Therapy groups now are reconstituting the family !!

Physical (not always sexual) contact --- people get the qualities of family contacts thru' these !

Bathrooms are needed for masturbation — that is the real need for privacy in these ......

Paul points out the imp. of his & my interrelation! as an important factor in this dialogue.. does not know what this will prove but somehow feels it is important .....

One conclusion is that crowding in an environment is usually a pleasant rather than an unpleasant quality. One thing I noticed after the discussion was that it seemed to focus a great deal on the needs & reactions of teen-agers - very apparent in Paul's comments - is this because that is when we formulate our strongest images of the environment? as it actually affects us rather than what we want it to be as a social characteristic?

PAUL BAUM
Nov. 15 · 67

1- Questions whether the rat sink hole
experiments on crowding have validity for us —
after all they get _no_ benefits at all from density —

2. What kind of spaces provoke violence
Hofer said people should not fear violence —
it is a creative force — if within some control.

3- A lot of solutions to life problems
occur outside family ... children need to watch
problems being solved ...... this is part of the
function of a family

4- The street is where you observe what
happens to other people
Work activities should be more visible
Adults should see what kids are doing.

This is A MEDEIVAL situation

ie: Paul keeps on
describing a close
but confined
inward looking
community.

SHAPE

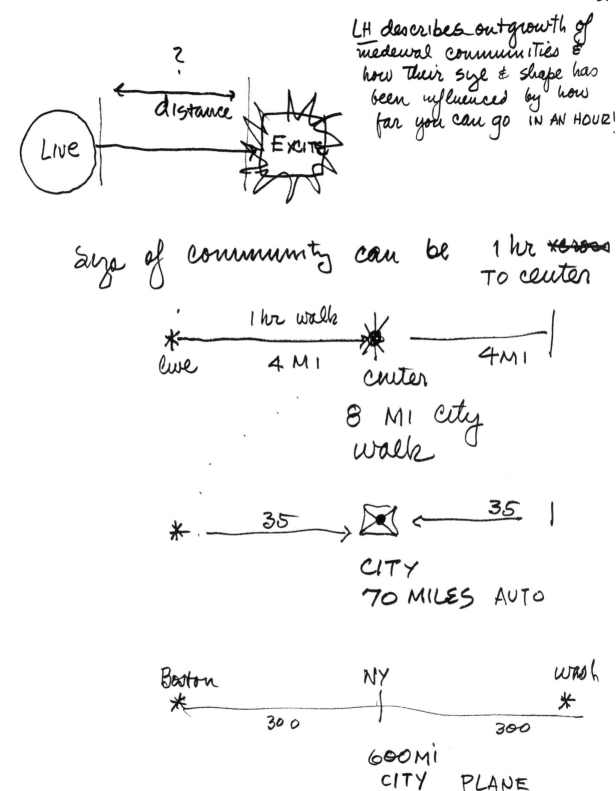

LH describes outgrowth of medieval communities & how their size & shape has been influenced by how far you can go IN AN HOUR!

? distance

Live

EXIT

Size of community can be 1 hr ~~across~~ TO center

1 hr walk
live   4 MI   center   4 MI

8 MI city walk

*   35   → ←   35 |

CITY
70 MILES AUTO

Boston   NY   Wash
*   300 | 300   *

600 MI
CITY   PLANE

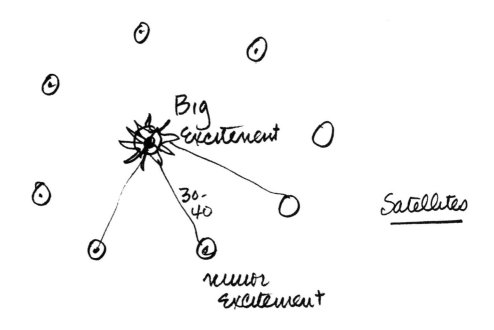

idea that you have to go somewhere
else for excitement should be questioned
Paul says when people get healthier they
can find it within themselves —
Boredom is not nothingness but
too great amount of self control -

Housing can be thought of either as a haven
or as a source of excitement!

Question — Is the pattern we are
looking for a return to
simpler more structured family
groups ?? tribe ?

NEEDs of birth & protection of children
is the ultimate determinant - ~~either~~
(even in changing environment) now
trying to hold on to these basic needs.

How long should children be protected
by the family?

BIRTH

How long?
Paul says puberty

Does this have to relate to the family?
or will it change?

rushing in of
outside factors
Tv- movies,
transport etc.

village

city

megalopolis

Losing touch = more human isolation!

240

LH – Why do primitive societies have
complex & deep psychological problems
(which they have evolved a structure
to deal with (ie Navajo sand paintings)

Should we talk to Hofer? re this & other things

What we are all struggling for is
an INNER SENSE OF PRIDE ←

There are significantly more women in Therapy
–than males

This is partly becuz it is more acceptable
in women (exterior pressures + self image)

We should discuss more women's
relation to community form –
have emphasized Male

Women are really quite different from
Men.

If person does not change he is SICK
I have brought up the whole notion of
continual change as a major factor
in design.

Change & growth are necessary to growth!

In Therapy Change only occurs in
relation to a meaningful relationship.

SHORT RANGE vs LONG Range planning.
LH points out that these are often in direct conflict with each other
Paul thinks many of the errors of
planning is being non-consideration
of short-range

What kind of design affects vandalism
Fancy materials would be a mockery?
unfamiliar - aggressive reaction
inappropriate materials is like a social
message

Paul has been asking whether vandalism
isn't as much related to the appropriateness
of design materials & form as anything ie:
If things are approp. to a group situation
they will not be vandalysd.
This leads into the question of processes
of change and whether these are not
the most significant thing — Paul says
in therapy - they are...
ie: people must be convinced of &
related to the processes.

we come back to relation of the designer
to what happens as a vital & moving
part of the relationship. - - - - -

One time soon we should deal with the
relation of the users to the environment &
its open space & how it affects them
once its done!

246

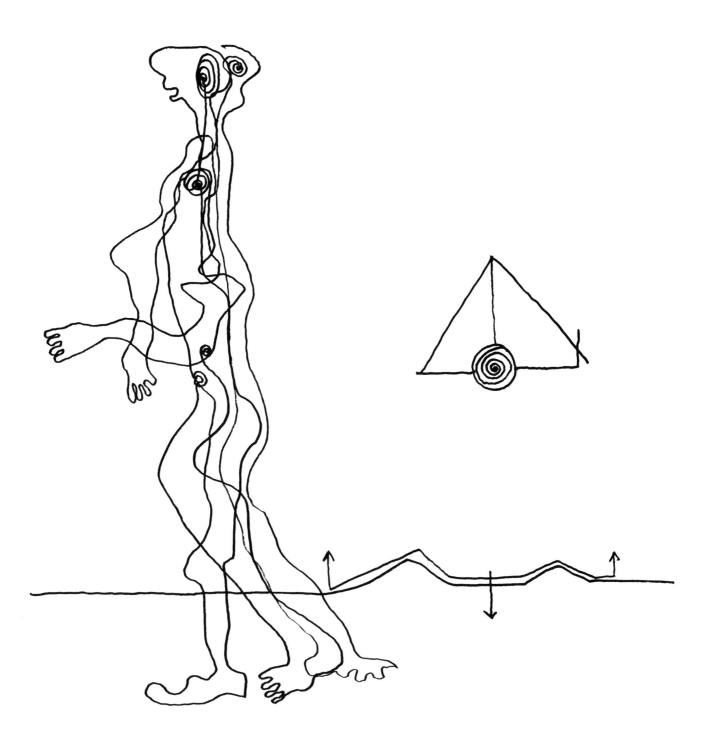

The need to establish a sense
of "SOME PLACE" - what does this mean?
(How does this differ or expand
Church's feeling - - ??)
Related is sense of identity which is
a crucial question for humans -
+ sense of pride..
See Hofers book - Ordeal of change -

Difference between Theatre & arch.
is that in arch. we make places
but people are on their own in
Theatre you bring in the people!

Paul thinks people should be involved in
the process of design - HOW - this is
crucial.
He does not mean advocate planning.
"   " mean unfinished projects allowing
for change

Example: lawns that tenants could
put in or things that tenants
can be involved in.

psychological distance ie: garbage
can or washing machines in
basement are not used - things
should not be too far away.
Distance would vary with people

ie: leave open-ended things they
can plug into.

partitions where they want them.
for example: some people would
want kitchen the largest room in
house.

Some would NOT want separate
bedrooms —

Flexibility !!

It may be much easier to design
flexibility and variety in out door
space — - .

How can a place be:

1 – Someplace

2. Not completely defined ...
allowing for participation

If not then will seem:

1 – Temporary to the people
ie: not the place but
peoples relation to it.

2 – Increase vandalism –

---

what are the levels of participation?

① Portland
Play places – Disneyland etc
Use & participate but not alter!

② Stores for potential use
but people alter to their
taste.

typical
shopping
center

③ allotment gardens in Europe.

④ movable features.

⑤ each individual designs his own place. ⑥ Build your own house

Analyze diff bet. pre-built tract house v.s. custom-built house - disc. of strains involved
Paul says this has to do with money. but I think it has to do with self image which in house becomes exposed.

We have decided that you want to allow all of this range of possib.

———————————————————

What image should we design for......?
Lower class want simple things :- jobs - improving their lot - power.

which kind of movie set?

Jews can <u>take</u> density - have always
    lived that way.

Trees and happy little children

Hofer feels you have to give people real
  sense (not phoney) of power :
    come up in the world !
    enhance functioning of family - <u>real</u> benefit.

    HOW ?

Must relate to functioning of family.
      Better ways of raising children
      enhanced Educ. facilities
      strengthen role of father !! which
        has been badly weakened.
      In poverty areas he can't get job.
      Don't see father functioning in
        predeful way

Is there some way for kids to see work
go on? not necessarily their own
fathers but _any_ man?

Interaction between living & working —

What elements should be in housing
areas..? answer: things which
raise people's ESTEEM
what's there will determine social life.
candy store, grocery store, promenade,

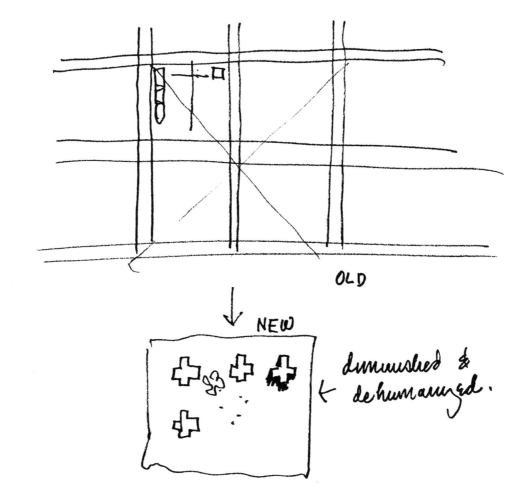

OLD

↓ NEW

diminished &
← dehumanized.

disorientation
difficult to relate to anything -
feeling of being a stranger - until I
got into someone's apartment -
No telephones around - very insecure -
far away from things ——————
Possibility of having various facilities at
different levels -

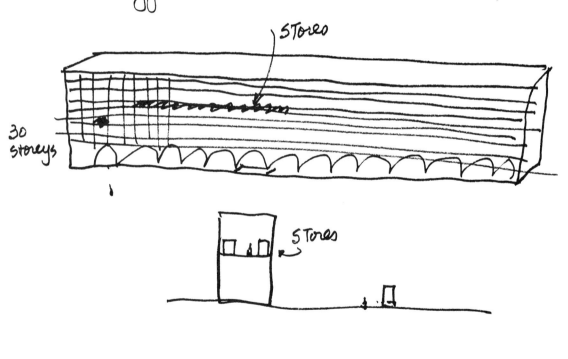

Stores

30 storeys

Stores

Stores

psychological neighborhood size - !
Draw your neighborhood =

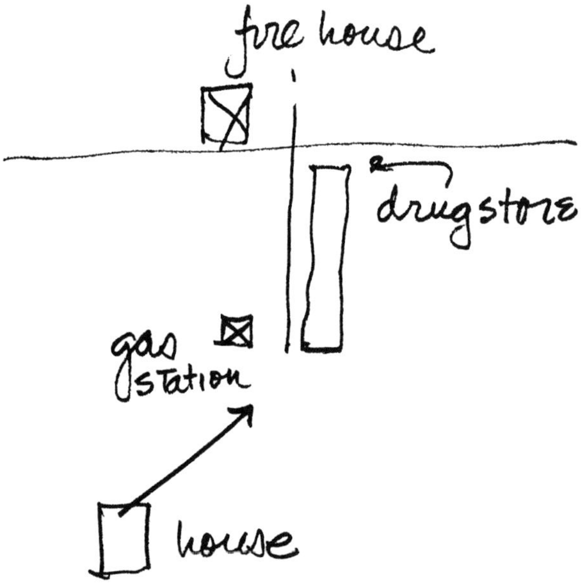

fire house

drugstore

gas
station

house

How would you like it to be?
we all became
anxious

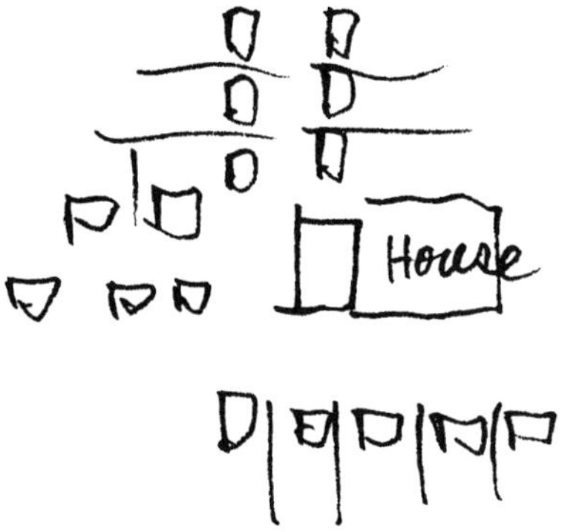

House

If actual neighborhood violates the
psychological neighborhood then resentment.

Continually referring to the close-in
feeling as desirable for city dwellers —
Source of this feeling is the FAMILY -
always looking to establish this feeling —
Paul feels this is a universal —
achieving it is various —
Can go to country in warm enclosure
or belong to groups....

Dick points out the difference of western
feeling of space - open - desert —
or car oriented -- filling station -
drive-in
feels uncomfortable in dense city like
San Francisco —

_____

another problem :—
            Draw the family !!

> Problems to give : ~~For~~ BECOME A GROUP!
> (one way to start is to start to become aware of yourself your own inner experience)

BECOME A FAMILY + (wow!)

Being a therapist is listening very carefully but being responsive.

1- Human needs . only come into focus when they are not met.

simple ○←——————————————————※ complex

physiological → safety → social → EGO → SELF
(only modifies   (self esteem)   Fulfillment
behavior when   respect of   includes
not met)   others)   growth

This system comes out of Abraham Maslow.

This system can apply to groups as well.

* People do want danger but want a mechanism to deal with it.

2- <u>THE FAMILY</u> —

Spouses need to form coalition & capable of transmitting instrumentally useful ways of adaptation useful to the society in which they live! ......

Persons relation to group & society recapitulate relation in family.

<u>NOTE:</u> In ghetto families abandonment by male
→ of family is only way they can support their families!

<u>DISRUPT NOW!</u> a technique to get people reacting & setting up group organizations. ..

Even rediculous things just to get things stirred up.

This is antithetical to what most management people want - ie: no community involvement or groups...

Paul emphasizes again the importance
of group involvement - also has as
a byproduct learning in group
situation.

A Tenderloin deotrict should be concentrated
(this is around Penn Sta) if you
move them where do they go to! You

USE OF OPEN SPACE - IT should
represent the life style of the community
must be multipurpose - not just
Tennis Courts - things & interaction
must occur - - -

But do not cut it off from rest of
community so they can interract......

In lower class housing focus the
life of the community internally
like: pool hall - small store
front churches.

This is a therapeutic orientation....

ie: do NOT change the life style.

Make the beauty not middle class
image!

If you relate to people in a meaningful way — "where they are" Not with the intention of changing them - - -

(Paul says do <u>not</u> change them even if they want to be changed - this is a trap)

If change is to occur they <u>must</u> do the changing.

WHAT YOU should do is encourage VISIBILITY - - -

after people have fully disclosed where they are ie: visibility then they can go on . . . .

How to get this across ?

←——————————————→

One suggestion

Make series of outlandish proposals

ie: ① No more babies allowed
Example in any housing project.

② Publish in press

③ Public outcry

④ AT interview suggest
No more love making —
~~public~~ punishable by
removing offenders from
project

↓

Press

PAUL BAUM
DEC 20

Paul would like to set up a
research group. like an "encounter group"
To study the real needs?

How about on weekend. This would
give fast reactions

WHERE?   in the environment.

COMPOSITION
- housewife
- cop or fuzz
- pusher
- KIDS
- Druggist, liquor, pool hall
-        minister
- Designer -- 2.
- Bewrocrat __

focus must be an Encounter !!
    Pull out stops...
allow free floating atmosphere — move around.

    around JAN 10.

selection of participants is important !
    Paul will inform us.

JAN 68 NEW PATTERN FOR NEW YORK

- urban open
  SPACE STUDY
  · NY NY ·

These run along the avenues

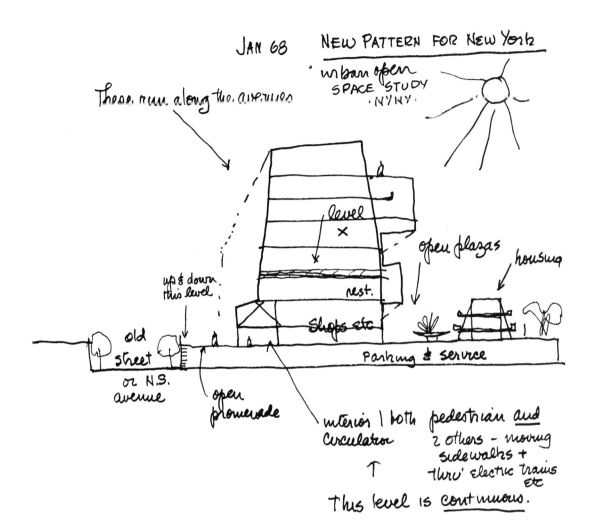

level ×

open plazas

housing

up & down.
this level

rest.

Shops etc

old
street
or N.S.
avenue

open
promenade

interior | both pedestrian **and**
circulation   2 others – moving
                    sidewalks +
            ↑   thru' electric trains
                              etc

Parking & service

This level is **continuous**.

The tower parts are **discontinuous**

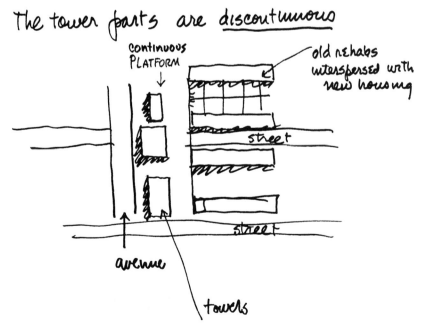

continuous
PLATFORM

old rehabs
interspersed with
new housing

street

street

avenue

towers

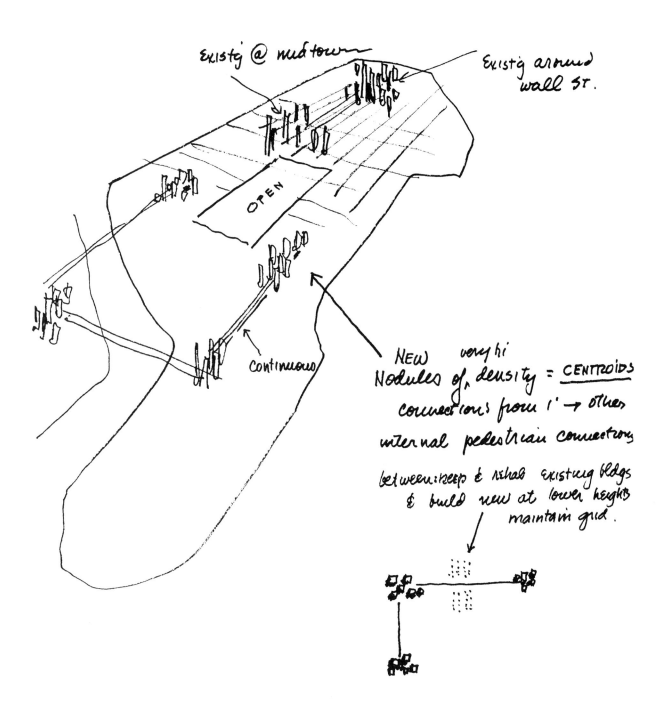

Existg @ midtown

Existg around wall St.

OPEN

Continuous

NEW   very hi
Nodules of density = CENTROIDS
connections from 1' → other
internal pedestrian connections

between: keep & rehab existing bldgs
& build new at lower heights
maintain grid.

January
1968

Sea Ranch
March 24.

Dana
May-'68

IN RETROSPECT — THE Trip ◁

- NOT in any order -

In general I am surprised by the virgin Islands
The land itself is not nearly as beautiful as I
had thought it would be. Foliage is low - not
many big trees (except in the rain forest &
down in some of the guts) and even the land
forms themselves are not very powerful. Inevitably
you must compare the V.I's with other similar
island landscapes -- Hawaii is much more
spectacular the hills more sculptural the rain
forest more lush - the running water much
more evident - The South Sea Islands that
I remember from Navy times also -- much
more lush & tropical.

    This is really dry and subtropical - much
more like Israel than Hawaii - dryer rather than
humid.....

    The hillsides remind me a great deal
of home - they are covered with chapparal-like
growth - much like the bay area. hills are about
the same, soil types are similar - convolutions
similar. I gather the normal rainfall pattern is
the same as Marin Co -- 40"/year tho' the

past few years have been about 20" which
is more like Jerusalem.

In general the whole impact for me is
much like the Mediterranean — Israel, the Greek
Islands — the scarcity of water, the cisterns, the
limestone hills, the climate... or like California

Maybe some of the errors in planning — some
of the erroneous "quality determinations" have been in
equating these Islands with the Tropics or even with
the Florida syndrome which seems to me very
different.

BUT→ The unique quality of course is the water
side of the islands and where it meets the land.
The beaches — where they exist — are simply superb —
nothing quite matches them — the water is
incredibly beautiful, the underwater reefs & the
underwater life is just as magnificent as it
can bee — the water temperature is just right — the
salinity is not overpowering... my finest times
were swimming in or under the water — I'd
like to come down if only to do that — — — —
water color is magnificent — clarity, transparency
the coral reefs the fish etc etc. wow!

The other really unique feature is the people — who
are handsome & beautiful and friendly and jolly

The big confrontations are between development & progress and all this implies and the qualities of the Islands. As Stewart Udall has said the valuable parts of the Island are extremely fragile ie: the beaches & the water.

It seems to me there are several searing issues...

1— The _suburbanization_ of the islands seems to me paramount. This is of course the **problem** of _all_ of America. Everyone on his own ½ acre in a little (or big for that matter) ranch house — The big costly ones are destroying the Islands more than the **little** ones. If this suburbanizing tendency continues you can have the Virgin Islands — I wouldn't want them ... a greyness where houses **gobble** up the land not close enough to make a real village or fare enough apart to make estates — the worst of both worlds rather than the best ... ugh!!

I don't know who is most at fault in this but probably everyone — the natives who want their "own" home — the New Yorkers who are "Levitt owning" the islands or the romantic rich who are bastardizing their

The Florida or L.A. Syndrome

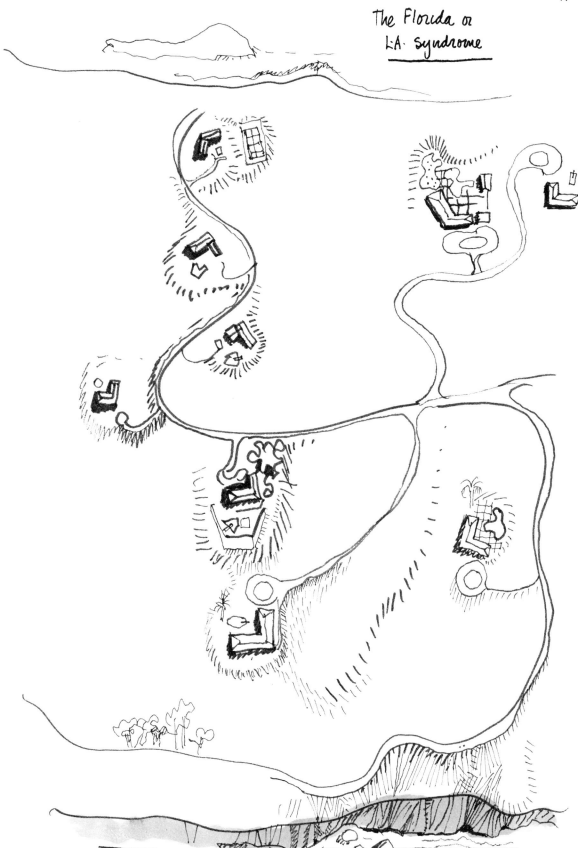

The Danes knew better than this — their "great houses" stood 4 sq on the estates and then the towns were tightly knit & dense - climbing up the hill-sides in an orderly pattern of streets, retaining walls, ramps, courtyards & decks. Not scatteration destroying the landscape but organic density which if anything enhances it. This form of living on the land in dense clusters can be seen at Charlotte Amalie or Christiansted. It is very Mediterranean. see the greek Islands .. Mykonos or any of the others --- something which I believe we need to apply as a principle .... this is what we tried to do in principle at the Sea Ranch -- Cluster rather than scatter!

2- The LOSS OF LAND & beaches to private development --- This is no different than the California coastline - all the big developers buy up prime land - including beaches & sell it off in parcels thus blocking access to the beaches. Land is expensive - $10-$20,000 + per 1/4 acre house lot. But because

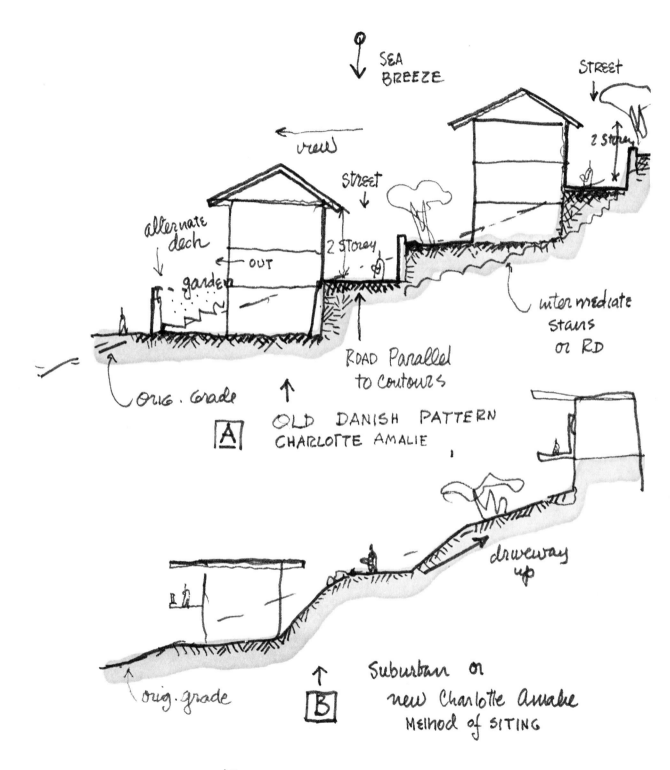

SEA BREEZE

STREET

view

STREET

2 storey

alternate deck

OUT

2 storey

garden

ROAD parallel to contours

intermediate stairs or RD

Orig. Grade

A OLD DANISH PATTERN CHARLOTTE AMALIE

driveway up

orig. grade

B Suburban or new Charlotte Amalie Method of siting

TWO DIFFERENT TECHNIQUES OF SITING BUILDINGS - Charlotte Amalie

there is so little land & really not too many sand beaches it becomes extremely critical. By now of course all land has become so inflated in value that it is hard for government to acquire it in any large amounts --- still this must be done.

NOTE: Why should land accrue in value for someone who has simply bought it & waited for it to make him rich? Primarily because of its scarcity value which he hasn't done anything about. We should try a system where all land starts at a common value & everyone benefits from development no matter where it occurs --- that way you could develop where development should occur - keep open where openness should be without the pressures of private entrepreneurs to squeeze everything possible out of their own land. Is that "Henry Georgism?"

3- <u>P</u>OPULATION INCREASE . I gather this is enormous - 20% per yr. partly from other Islands where alien bonded labor is brought in to do what is considered menial work & partly influx from the mainland . The 2 have different impacts but the result is the same - increasing build-up of structures . The Native (read Negro) increase produces suburbs & little ticky-tackies like Sydney Kessler does or the public housing authority and the mainlanders scatter ranch-houses. In either case the Islands are beginning to be inundated.

4 - <u>Increasing urbanization</u> - This is particularly noticeable on ST. THOMAS but beginning on ST. CROIX. Automobile traffic is almost Manhattan-like in an area boxed in by the waterfront & the hills to the North. There is really no possible bypass solution at Charlotte Amalie - there will have to be much better (ie: since there's hardly any mass transport)- parking structures, pedestrian zones in the downtown area etc. etc. ie: all the solutions must be applied here for the same reason as in the overcrowded cores of mainland cities.

But urbanism must also include techniques of building which will be dense - without being High, I suspect, so that the horrible fracturing off at the edges that is occurring uphill in the newer sections of Charlotte Amalie does not occur any more --- see the 2 sections of the old & new Charlotte Amalie....

Also the lowlands are beginning to get covered with industrial structures which are eating up land - terribly unpleasant to look at. & cause a great deal of Noise up on the hillsides. I was very aware of this at Henry's - the close in view is really a mess - the hillside views are getting clobbered, the roof of the Hilton hotel is a MASS (mess) of airconditioning equipment and the NOISE from the flat area below is very annoying.....

5. AIRPORT —

I'm not an airport expert & therefore cannot really evaluate the feasibility of improving, or changing the direction of the runway at TRUMAN. There is a danger becuz of the short runway & the college is NOISY.

My trip out to see the proposed airport site with the governor was revealing. Tho' much of the mangrove lagoon will be left physically there is NO question in my mind that the impact of the airport will destroy it visually & psychologically. In addition NO Body realizes the proliferation of facilities implied in this development ..... there will be a lot of knocking down of hills - vast areas will be required for airport structures, terminals, service facilities, parking for cars entrance roads, maintenance sheds etc etc. In addition a major road

connection will be required. Motels & other
facilities will spring up. That end of the island
will become very urbanized.

The cays will be destroyed and the
barrier reef obliterated.

In the last analysis however the Islands are beautiful and well worth trying to save. The water & beaches on St. Johns — the spectacular undersea trails at Buck Island, the harbor at Christiansted, the old parts of all 3 towns are superb.......... the North East side of St Thomas is still untouched & the view down that Coast is as spectacular as any in the world. !!!

St Croix has great charm in its older sections & the confrontation between the 19th & 20th century is very apparent here. I am confused by the lack of Agriculture — there are vast flat plains formerly in Sugar & Cotton now completely fallow.. in Israel these areas would be producing crops. I can't see that they can remain fallow but what happens if they urbanize?

Joe Brown has St. John well in hand -- but he needs money to buy up as many of the in-holding properties as possible — particularly up on the ridges and where development will destroy the qualities of the park, also something MUST be done about the qualities & character of Cruz Bay. The whole of St. John's is beautiful & my memory of the beaches there — it seems a long time ago even tho' only a week — are they are some of the most beautiful in the whole world -- Caneel bay certainly one of the finest resorts - Trunk bay magnificent - Hurricane hole, Lameshur beach --- superb!

In summary my impression is of an enormous tension between Islands of great beauty, beaches and lagoons unmatched anywhere and the demands of progress. It is quite clear to me that as much land and water should be preserved as pure unoccupied open space as possible...... how much will be, of course, a function both of available funds and a determination of what precisely should be acquired.

But the most difficult problem will - even so - remain!! And that is how people in increasing numbers can settle on what remains and Enhance it rather than destroy it. I keep thinking in my minds eye of the old Towns - Charlotte Amalie, Christansted, Frederichsted and how full of charm & character they are. I think of the Greek Islands and the mediterranean coastal towns and how magnificently they Enhance rather than destroying the landscape.

We need to find our own NEW techniques to achieve these qualities in the virgin Islands before it is too late.

I think it can be done. I expect it will require

Education as well as laws; desire as well
as instruction; motivation as well as architectural
controls and good planning.

Concepts of SPACE - LH discussion······

OF THE VISUAL ARTS···

Painting has tradit. dealt with the representation of space in 2 dimensions

Sculpture has dealt with space which you look at from outside.

DANCE has dealt with motion through & in space.

~~space~~ Engineering - structures as objects in space

[arch] has in its greatest forms attempted to orchestrate these into structures within which events can happen. modulating spaces also for functional purposes

Functions can be either real or symbolic··
            Temples. palaces.
            or ballrooms···

But marriage of 2 = arch. — very seldom achieved
arch → Landscape arch → city planning → regional planning.

SPACE as a physical enclosure
Form follows function - Sullivan (earlier goodnough)
Less is More - MEIS
Form follows program
The program is an expression of
        deep seated actual + unexpressed desires including the site
        arch = community.

YIN - YANG   attitude about space

arch enclose space . . . . .

 "   within space . . . .

 "   responding to space

 "   going against "

The first statement is a violation !

Land comes first . . . first impact is like a rape

The reconstitution of wholeness —

   growth → new fruition . . . .

Types of space -

   Renaissace

   Baroque

   Medieval

   Japanese

 Et. gothic

Ethnic variations in space :

Defining space   -   Klee - Barsch & others

   simplest pt = dot   •

   dot ⟶ Line —

   line ⟶ plane ☐

   plane ⟶

Extension of the dot —
person — Earth — capsule
S/R ⟶ SF trip moving dot -

$\boxed{\text{heirarchies of space}}$ } -

Near space   0 - 2 ft
Midspace   2 - 16 ft.
far space   17 - 30 feet
Remote space   30 ⟶ ∞

<u>physical</u>   <u>cognitive</u>

Sierra -
aug 28 - 68 -

Pn

possible wall for
Portland fountain

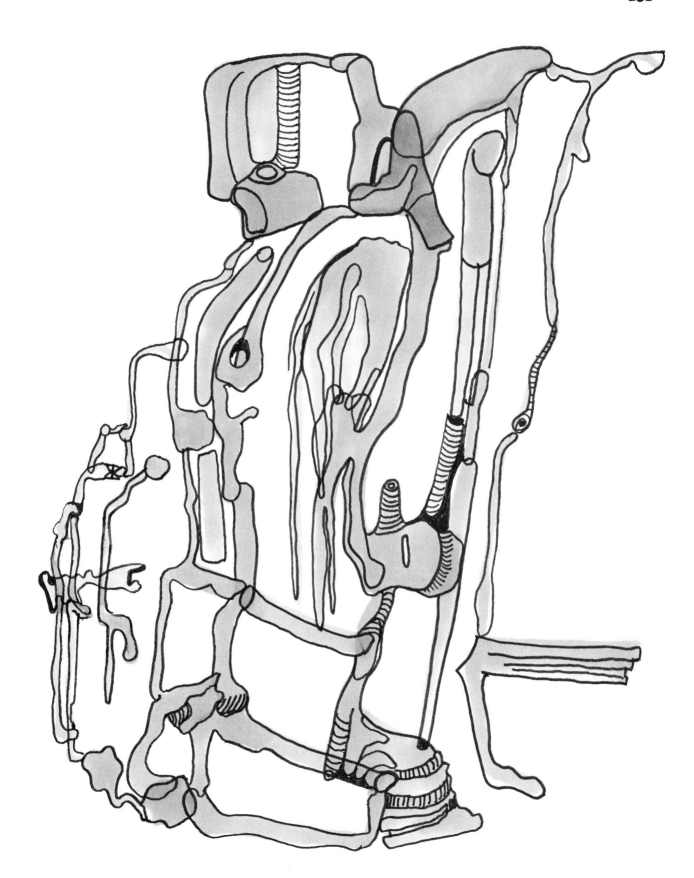

<u>NOTE</u> TO myself: · ▪ Forget how people will <u>use</u> the book or building in Systems for organization.

▪ Do not worry about one step following the other or relating to what's before & what is after.

▪ Avoid like the plague the goal making but ie:
If they and <u>after</u> they have read the book then They can understand the environmental problem They will know what to do about it.

Do the book from <u>within</u> - telling what you are interested in and how you have discovered things

Talk about <u>SCORING</u> which to you means ways of ordering events taking into account people & environments <u>and</u> the whole question of <u>WHAT</u> you order and <u>HOW MUCH</u> you order ... and what you do not order.

Tell about the relation of <u>SCORING</u> to large scale planning of urbs and regions Talk about this in terms of Sea Ranch & YBC & Hennepin & ultimately of the VI project & what you are trying to do there ie: "balance forces"

Tell about the regional landscape and how it needs to bring into some sort of balance natural forces, preservation of open spaces and at the same time allowing people to enter into it & interact LIVE etc in it.

Disclose the essential characteristic of the oecological attitude ie: *that natural forces are their own determinants (as well as are aesthetic ones) and how you go about finding these (+ cultural & topographic and whatever to serve as the basis of a Score to disclose what should happen on land.

Deal with the issue raised the other nite at Fauge's talk ie: the architect — urban designer is a specialist who knows more about space than the layman and my feeling that where we are in deep trouble is this very attitude and that is the important meaning of "audience participation" ie: feedback & group design = community . . .

NOTE re: Communications →

How to say the things we need
to say in phrases and idioms
that are understandable - a
translation is required not only
in language, from our professional
jargonese, BUT more importantly
into modes of thinking.

EXAMPLE: On PBY Antilles airboat Trip
from ST. Croix → ST. Thomas I was
asked a question by a young man
re: our waterfront proposals. launched
into a long explanation .. finally
he felt he understood + said
"OH you mean there exists a problem
which must be solved"!

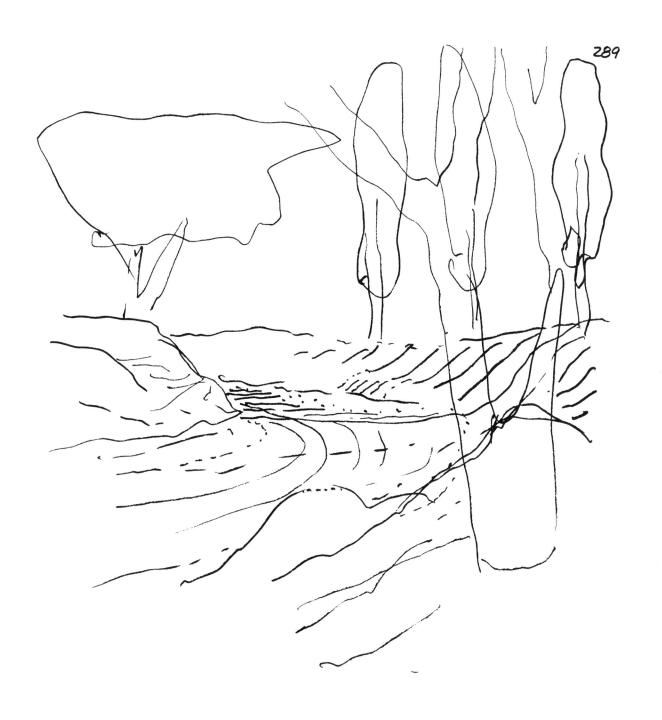

Corte Madera Creek
below College Ave bridge
after first pass by corps
of engineers...

TAM creek
CM "
flood control
april 20

The Classical confrontation:

CORPS - vs. CITIZENS.
of ENGINEERS

abstract notion   vs.   specific desire to keep
of linear approach   aesthetic & oecological
to Flood Control   qualities.

linear approach Ends   combination of values
up more costly rather   probably Ends up with
than less doing more   less cost but requires
than is need   more subtelty of planning

conc box requires   RIP-RAR more flexible
geometrical alignment.   in alignment both vert
vertical walls loss   & horiz - less damage
of trees fence along   to trees - no fence requires
top no modification
to alignment is possible

Run at an oecological scoring technique (flight to Denver) June 16 -

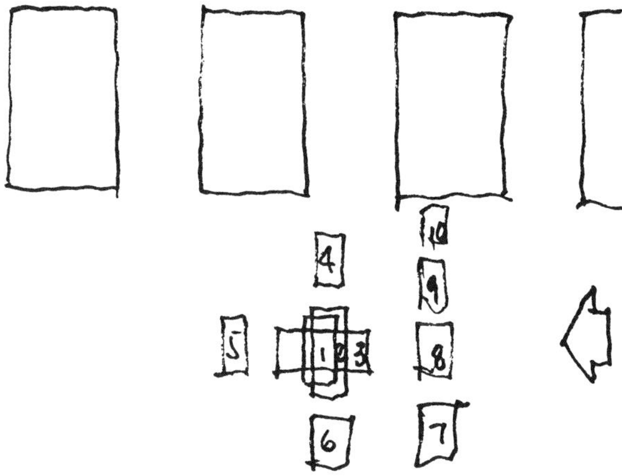

TAROT

usual sequence of "throwing"

How about a similar system for the oecological "throw"?

linear ▪▪▪▪

+

or the EE Ching hexagram?

Each card a major factor ie:

drainage
soil
wind

etc. give symbol

1. 1st throw all cards to evoke a general image of the oecol. situation

2. 2nd throw cards on the SITE MAP. where they apply. stack if necessary.

3. 3rd Throw a development pattern

↕ these have to be related HOW?

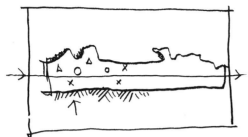

this means OUT.

possible format for cards ie: draw out the site for
each card & then establish symbols for each ~~oec~~ situation —

X ⊙ △ ▽ ⌣ ← ∿∿→ whatever

or

wind drain soils etc

100

0

Another possibility for an oecological
scoring method using the I CHING (hexagram)
method .... for example the 8 FU-HSI
trigrams

KHIEN   TUI   LI   Kàn

SKY   water   sun   Thunder

SUN   KHAN   Kǎn   Khwan

wind   rain   mountain   earth

Each one of these sets has subsets ie:
fr. example TUI also means marsh or lake

(NOTE → check with Tom Thorpe the technique used
by oecologists for mapping)

294

R.H = Rana
@ Sea Ranch
Sept 2.

DEAR { DON
SAT
VIG
Jerry
LARRY

FRIDAY
NOV 13th '69

My interpretation of where we are
at in the office bases itself on a deep
sense that everything that people are
saying at all levels is valid and we need
to take affirmative and strong action.
Much of what has been said has been hinted at
often said before — BUT NOW I get a great
sense of urgency and one feels Hostility. becuz
I feel people feel that nothing is really
going to happen or that it will be too LITTIE
and too late.

I sense a feeling of a need for revolution
& that what is being offered by us is "accomadation."

As a diagram I have outlined
the office's history & development in the
following way : —

⟶

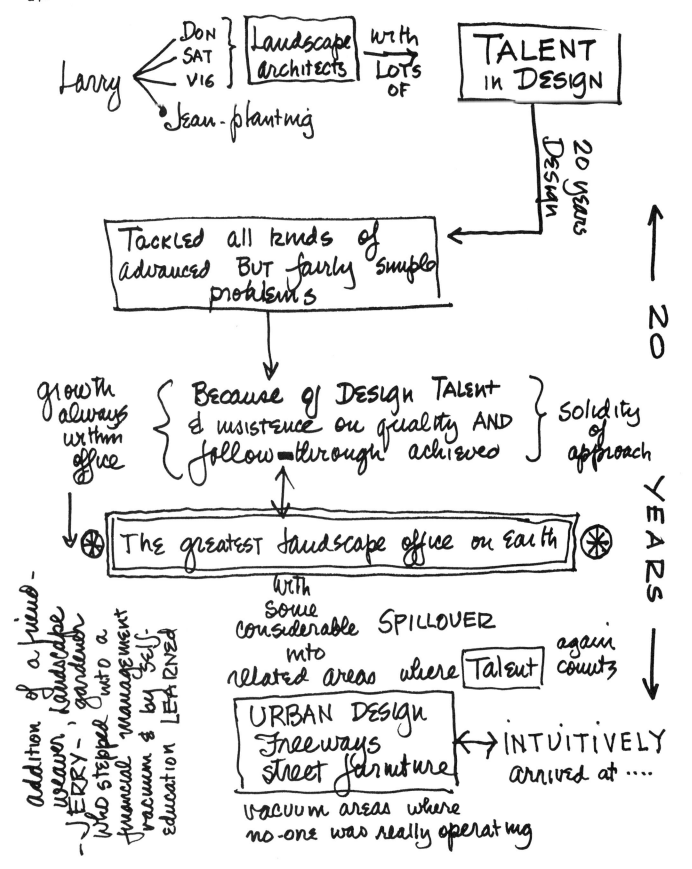

296

Larry ← Landscape architects (DON / SAT / VIS) with LOTS OF

Jean-planting

TALENT in DESIGN

20 years Design

Tackled all kinds of advanced BUT fairly simple problems

growth always within office

{ Because of DESIGN TALENT & insistence on quality AND follow-through achieved }

Solidity of approach

The greatest landscape office on Earth

with some considerable SPILLOVER into related areas where [Talent] again counts

20 YEARS

addition of a friend - weaver, landscape JERRY -, gardener who stepped into a financial management vacuum & by self-education LEARNED

URBAN DESIGN freeways street furniture ←→ INTUITIVELY arrived at ....

vacuum areas where no-one was really operating

This has produced works of all kinds of great beauty - some important prototypes, & an image of a great & Talented office which is working creatwely in many new fields & IS FUN TO BE IN.....

One major breakthrough on a Non-design oriented level was an early interest in and work on oecology as a guiding force in design... For perhaps the same reason as everything else this arm has not developed beyond a "tool for design" & on a Micro-regional level rather than MACRO-regional.. ie: it has never really developed as it could (& still might) into an Ecological planning department in the Eastern sense....

For the rest we have been solidly based in DESIGN, intuition, & QUALITY CONTROL has been very high..... very little if any on research or new techniques, or new approaches or social issues and the office structure has reflected this

Quality control

DESIGNers PRINCIPALS

associates

STAFF

1:1 ratio
1:1 basis

298

And this control system has applied to all problems we have tackled → even including those which **BY** <u>aptitude or training</u> the principals as designers have had very little knowledge OF. This even was applied to finances, administration hiring, personnel problems etc. etc.

This ^approach has been both a great strength & a great weakness......

IT has, to a large degree, reflected L.H.'s biases and hang-ups ie: ① never really trust anyone who isn't a brilliant designer

② Always work with people <u>within</u> the organization & assume they can take on additional tasks... & solve them rather than bringing in people from outside to tackle problems.....

This ^attitude has been a source of strength because it allowed for organic growth & produced a uniform & agreed upon <u>SET OF VALUES</u> but it has at the same moment limited input & tended to become ingrown & prevented diversity of approaches. It has limited our creativity to what WE COULD

ourselves bring to problems IE:
our own limitations (or strengths) became
identical with our organization which is
another way of saying

→ LH & ASSOC. IS US ←

(with limited input from outside)

Having said that we have designed &
described LH & Assoc as in our own image
Lands. arch Design oriented based on intuitive
talent with us leading & controlling design in
a heirarchical system which it parallels
both in professionalism AND organization
one a mirror image of the OTHER.

BUT

comes the revolution & I hope we're ready
for it. And the revolution is in – NEED, &
life style, and motivation, more than in
SCORE. It is not so much the score
which is under attack as the R
IE: the parameters of LH & Associates.

a whole new group of Associates
have now been merged into the system

many of whom are architects, some are not
brilliant designers but whose interests lie
elsewhere — many of whom are reaching in
new directions which do not put DESIGN
(& particularly landscape DESIGN) at the head
of the hierarchy of values or motivations...

This is neither a mirror of ourselves
Nor in OUR image
" " " particular area
of competence

IT even leaves us out as being
in charge

Every element which does NOT put DESIGN
as the primary value leaves us only part
of the team & not leading. Nor do
associates or staff for that matter see why
we should be at the top of the DECISION
making hierarchy in areas where our
competence is not unique

DESIGN — Yes
other things — Why? even NO!

& that includes administration where
they and we all agree that we are
lacking in SKILL or interest or both.

STAFF I gather feels all the above + other hang-ups & frustrations. Many of them consider themselves at least the equal of associates in DESIGN & since more recently out of school more "UP" on what's going on than both Associates & Principals.... they all read more, are bright & bushy tailed and LESS willing to submerge their own feelings to "getting along" or "going UP." They are also less willing to cover up.

In addition they are all here because of the image of the office AS (To go back To) the beginning)

❀ | "The greatest OFFICE in the world" | ❀

partly because of the workshops, I think, & articles & word of mouth they believe we really "SWING" & are working with intensity on brilliant projects — LOTS of dialogue with brilliant people — colorful — WOW!! And with social relevance. Sort of an exciting extension of graduate school

The reality is less than that
by too much!!

And it really _is_ less than that
Except at peak moments .... & they
aren't often enough to satisfy ⟵

So ⊕
↓

In my opinion there is great validity in
how ~~staff~~ _feels_ & how associates
feel.

I think principals have done as well
as they ~~possible~~ _could_ within the configuration
of their own interests, motivations, particular
talents & life styles & their feelings are _valid_

I believe we need to find ways to
score out ways through LH & assoc. to
accomodate all these needs. I feel it
can be done but I believe it requires
breaking the mold. The mold & the
hang up is

DESIGN (traditionally seen as
form making & particularly
landscape

IN-HOUSE upward mobility to solve
problems

1 - I feel we will be unable to solve the organizational set up through the sole efforts of the Principals & that we need an outside objective person working with & for us for 1-2 years to structure us in response to where we want to go.

2 - I believe "DESIGN" ~~must~~ can move sideways & not CAP the hierarchy while enrichening us.

There are other equally important subjects & areas of interest for us to involve ourselves in...

Planning
Ecology   } are among them
Urbanism
Social issue

Personally — for me
    Education - both internal } are
                  External   } important

also other media
    Films, TV, articles etc etc.

Social relevance crops up over & over again but what this means is unclear... in the limited sense it cannot mean just working in the ghetto... it <u>can</u> involve pollution, ecology, significant planning breakthroughs as well. Often its in the eye of the beholder... I think we need to have dialogue on this.

I think we need to score finances only because without them we will cease to EXIST.

I think we need to encourage input from other people so as to grow & STOP LIMITING OURSELVES further BY OUR OWN LIMITATIONS

we need to break out of our own self-imposed closed system.

Larry

Lovejoy –
June 23–70

auditorium forecourt
opening day - June 23

KIT FOR urban design

make out of hardwood blocks

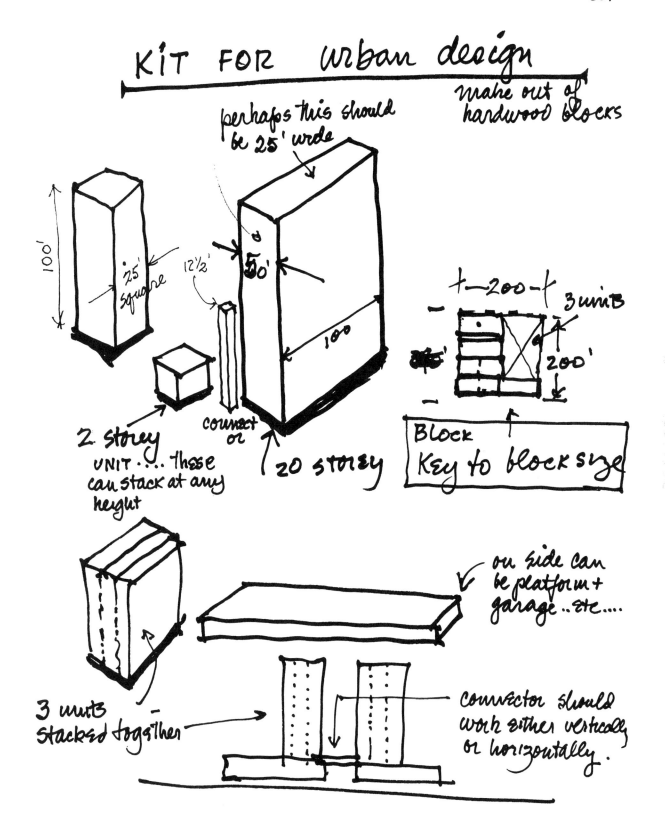

perhaps this should be 25' wide

100'

'25' square

12½'

50'

100

connector

2 storey

20 storey

UNIT .... these can stack at any height

↑—200—↑ 3 units

200'

Block

Key to block size

3 units stacked together

on side can be platform + garage ...etc....

connector should work either vertically or horizontally.

LINGUA FRANCA } urban design KIT - cont.

The Kit should be flexible to the extent that it does NOT predetermine or control the result either in form or concept .... but primarily in terms of the content ..... try different shapes

possible non limiting forms →

for nesting

or small units ☐ to make up So you dont preconceive hi-Rise solutions...

Exploration of these KITS as tools for urban design needs to be a major element in the summer workshop.....

OBJECTIVES vs GOALS

R under RSVP can be considered to include
OBJECTIVES but not ~~goals~~

The difference between the 2 is that GOALS
establish end products, results and the
(at least apparent) formalism of what
emerges from processes
OBJECTIVES do not indicate results or a
product nor have A form … they are
physically oriented MOTIVATIONS

We could say that in R?S a city plan
could may should have certain objectives
whereas goals would be ANTI-process since
not accepting of input & pluralism during
"running-out" of the score …..

OBJECTIVES are process-oriented
goals are product "

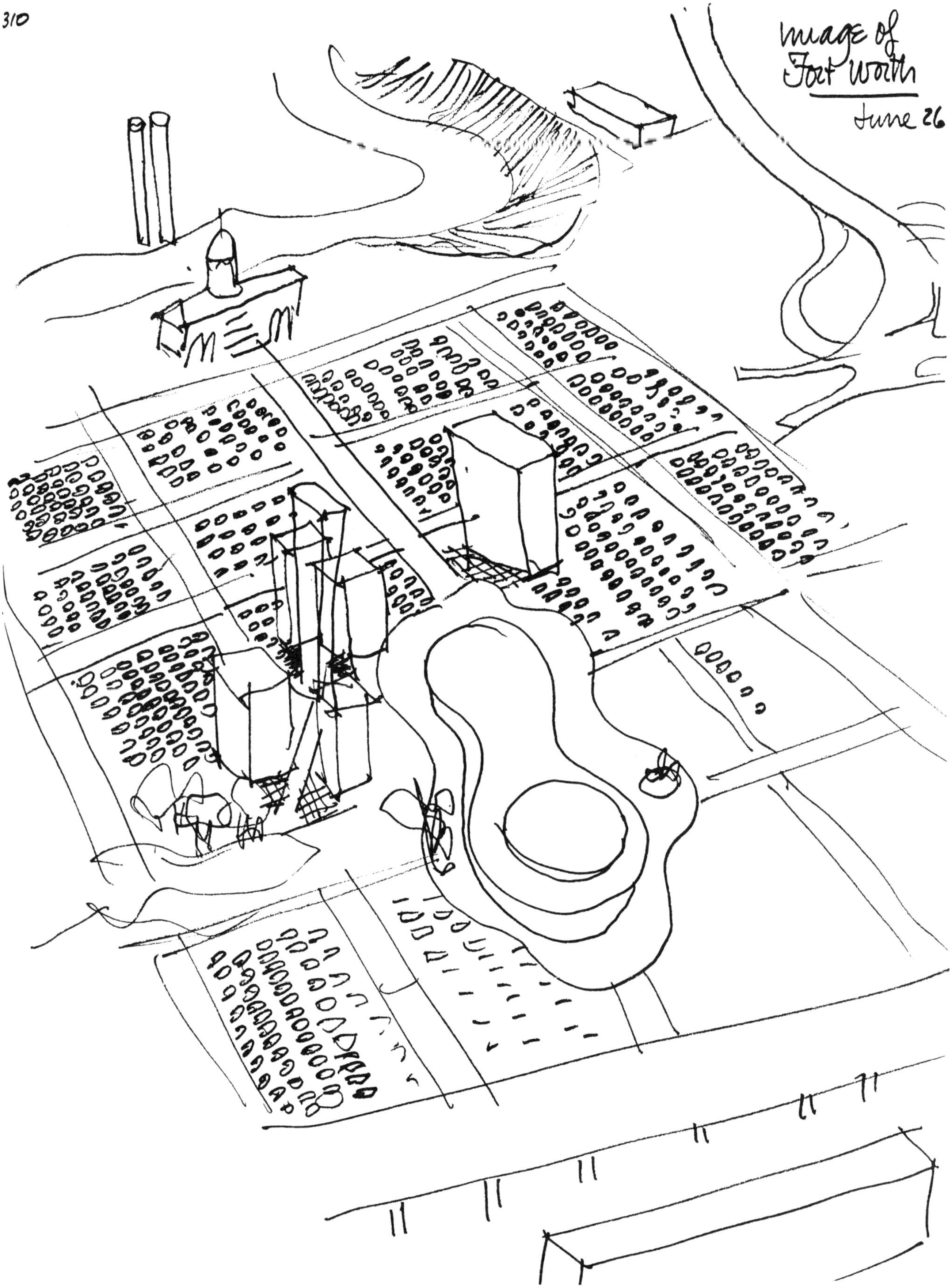
image of
Fort Worth
June 26

San Miguel Allende
July 2...
1970

THEORY:

Man & nature interface in an
integrated way when man works with
the same processes as nature : —

" COPIES her mode of operation
→ USES   NOT
her results ...... "

{ thus as an example the Japanese garden
is as artificial as the classical garden
But a city can be itself Natural as
a wood is .....

OR

in dance :   You cannot imitate a
birds but you can take on
birdlike characteristics ...

BASE THE ARTICLE
⇓   ON THIS

The Portland fountains are "natural" not because
they imitate nature but because the processes by
which natural effects of this kind operate have
been understood & recycled into an art form.
IE: form followed process   thus an interface
between man & nature arose in which we as
designers SCORED the process from which the
result emerged.

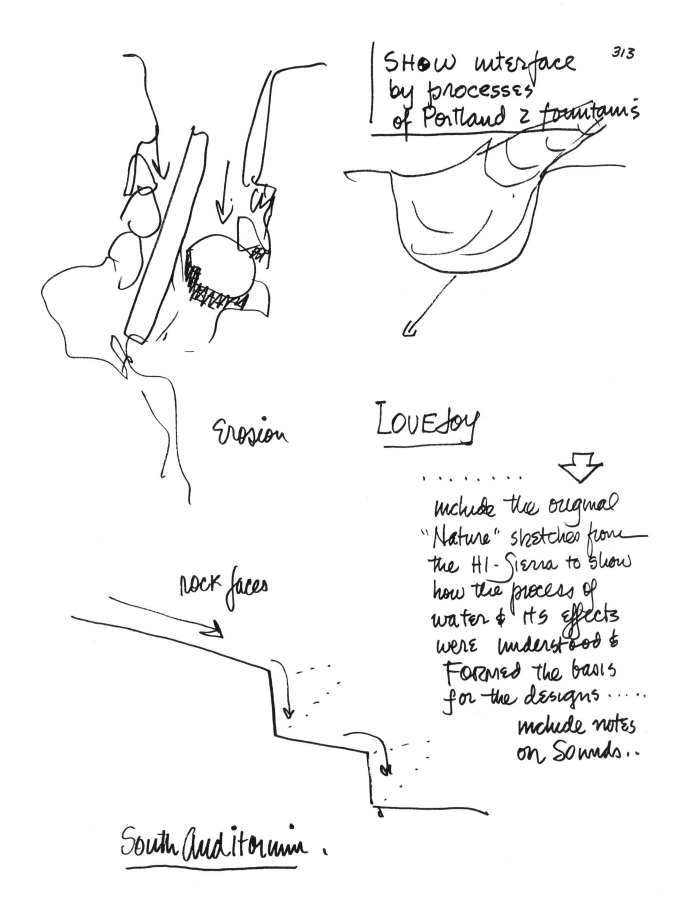

313

SHOW interface
by processes
of Portland 2 fountains

Erosion

LOVEJOY

include the original
"Nature" sketches from
the HI-Sierra to show
how the process of
water & its effects
were understood &
FORMED the basis
for the designs .....
include notes
on Sounds..

rock faces

South Auditorium .

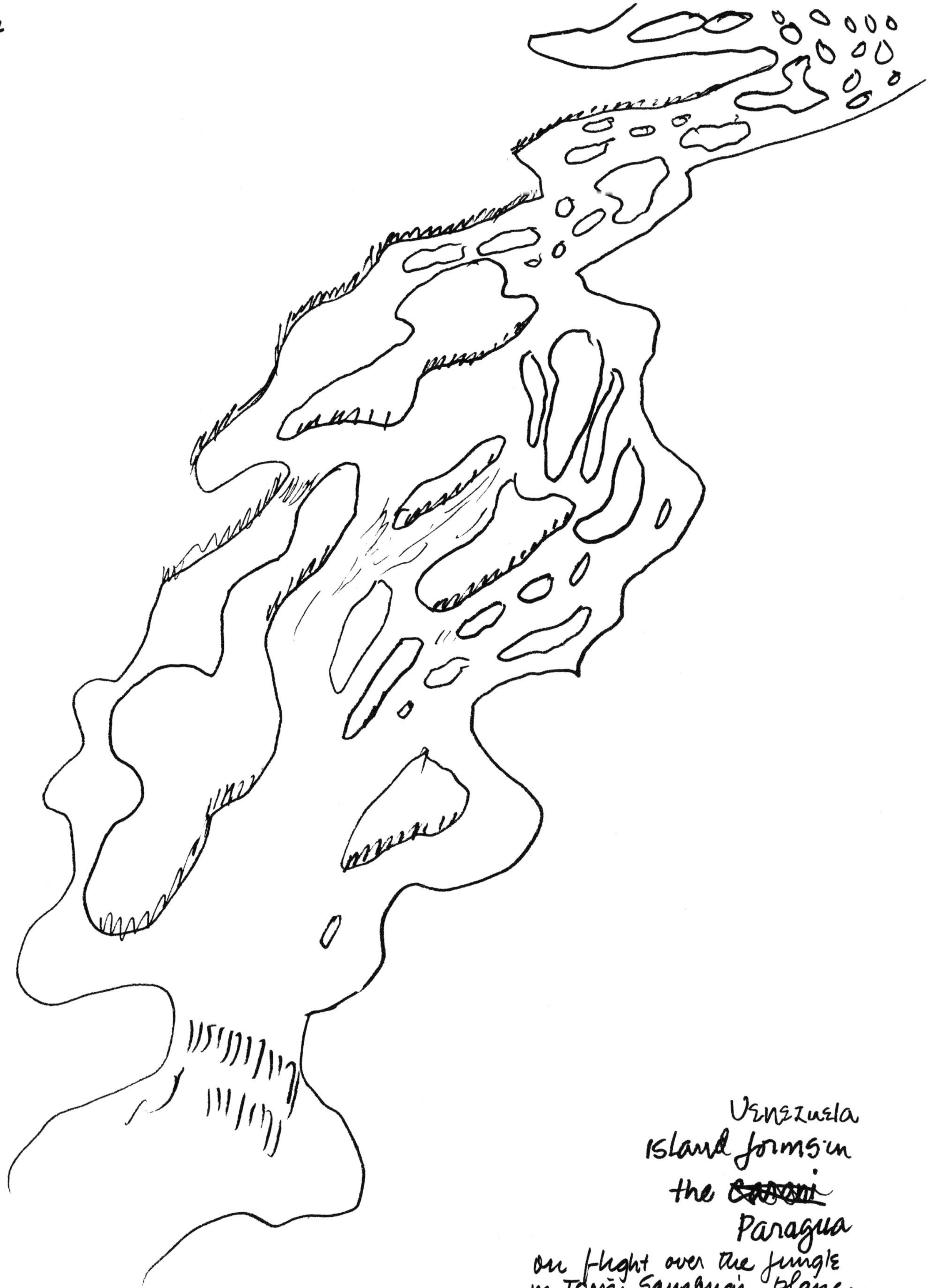

314

VENEZUELA
Island forms in
the ~~Caroni~~
Paragua
on flight over the jungle
in Tomás Sanabría's plane...

THE TRIP TO KANAVAYEN

This spectacular trip into the State of BOLIVAR brought home to me more clearly than I could have imagined the character of Venezuela... for one thing I realized (what I had been told before but had not focused on) how under developed vast areas of the country are... Other than the urbanized northern fringe the interior starting not far south east of the TUY valley is occupied first by a few scattered small cities & finally by the vast "llanos" area penetrated by some of the early new oil fields, some cattle & very little else 'til you reach the Orinoco) where around CIUDAD Bolivar & the new ciudad Guayana industrialization is well under way complete with dense layers of smog & a general feeling of energy and uglification which unfortunately in an industrialized age are 2 words which seem always to go together....

After flying S.E for 2 hours we turned due south into the tepuy area - an incredibly beautiful interior of great mesas sticking up out of jungles with meandering rivers and enormous waterfalls dropping from sheer cliffs. Angel Falls is the most amazing of course & it falls from

"Devils mountain" - over 3000 feet free fall
The trip in was difficult because of the clouds

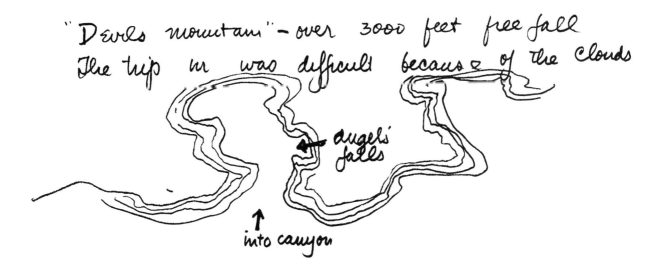

angels falls

↑
into canyon

and because the canyon in which the falls are
located is dead ended & somewhat like a keyhole
in shape & thus hard to find under a cloud
cover. But the whole area is laced by falls
of every size & description each unique & some
simply erupting out of the dense jungle....
Amongst the most spectacular is at Canaima
where approaching over the sluggish Caroni Rio
all of a sudden you drop over the falls which
are turbulent and the water just thunderous..
            area around Kavawayen
The whole ~~region~~ ^is uniquely beautiful
& ecologically fascinating.. the rivers are
coca-cola colored, the water has a low pH –
around 4.2 I'm told – the rocks are
sedimentary & very acidic ... there are few
insects, few birds, no fish hardly any animals..
(P.S. This does not hold around Canaima)

facts that were referred to over & over by the venezuelans who were with me altho' I was less conscious of this N of my experiences in the very Hi Sierra than they since it seemed similar in that regard to the wilderness areas I know (except for fish) But I gather compared to the llano area which is teeming with life this seems strange.

It would be fascinating to do a regional study of this area based on ecological principals & research AND a conscious need to keep its wilderness quality --- I am myself somewhat worried about their desire to "DEVELOP" the area for tourism ..... nothing (as we know) destroys a region more quickly than tourism, accessibility, hotels and development.. and the Indians & their culture could quickly disappear as apparently it already has begun to ...

The missions threw me back 400 years to the old Spanish notion of bringing light to the poor benighted savages. In complete defiance of the laws of ecology, of man and his inherent dignity — of the Indians own beautiful symbiotic relation to nature — these priests have the

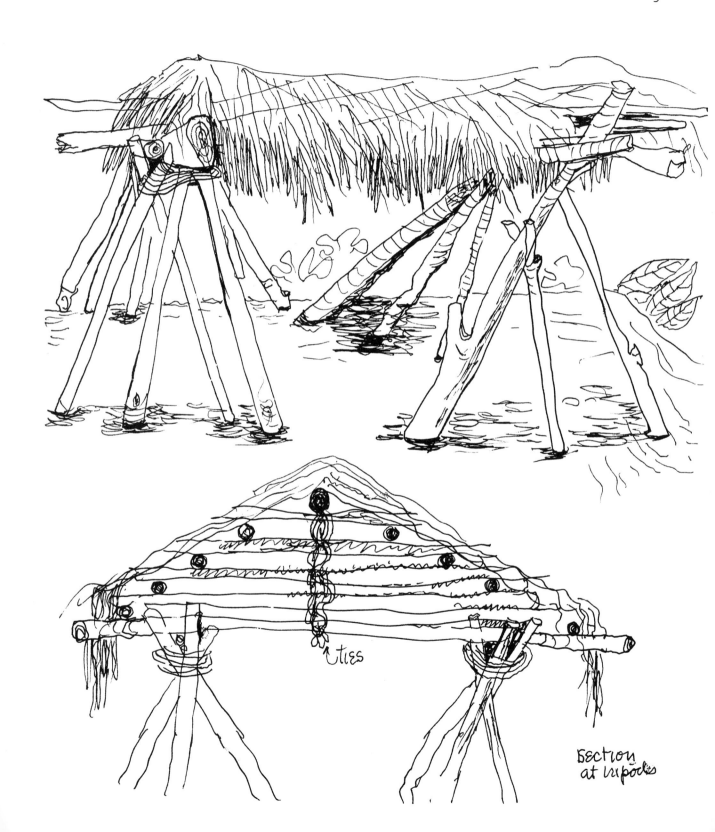

ties

Section
at tripods

what I would call audacity to destroy
a people and demean them .. in human
terms they are making groups of people
extinct & thrusting their own (or ours
perhaps is a better term since it is western
industrialized Society we are speaking of)
presumed
values upon a people who are completely lacking in
any defense against this invasion of their
privacy......

→ I would really want to engage in
a regional study of this whole area -
mounting a complex multi-disciplinary
team including anthropologists, sociologists
as well as environmentalists - ecologists....
The assignment of this group would be to
analyze the existing ecological (including the
human ecological) situation of the area, the
life styles of everything & then based on these
as a foundation develop OBJECTIVES & motivations
for the various divergent & often incompatible
groups.... Based on these R's scores
could be developed which would "run out"
a series of alternative ways of treating
the area all the way from (I would

presume) intensive development of the region
to very light touches perhaps in carefully
selected locations.... ~~Based on These~~
alternative SCORES <u>S</u> action could be
decided upon .. even including such decisions as
the simple one Martin & NIKKO want to carry
out of stocking the streams around <u>KANAVAYEN</u>
and planting a deer population for hunting....
<u>and</u> how to relate to the Indians which is
no less ecologically problematical to say
nothing of socially-culturally.....

    It is - incidentally - interesting that
the Indians in the Kanavayen area are called
<u>Pomones</u> .... our North Coast Indians around
Stewarts Point are POMOS .... we destroyed
the POMOS mostly by killing off altho' the
Russians at Fort Ross "used them" as slaves
as did the early Spaniards around SONOMA
& that destroyed many of them too & the
implications & probable results are similar
here ..... How to integrate a really primitive
group of people into an advancing technological
society without hurting their own "culture"
is a fascinating problem which could be
attempted here if it isn't already too late......
    (contin after transportation)

I notice that cars get "closer" to each other here than in U.S. less margin-of-error

---

→ continue re: trip to Kanavayen ←

The whole area needs to be evaluated as a National Park (probably NOT national Forest with its "multiple-use" implications) especially in an area which is apparently very rich in IRON ore & other minerals which could lead readily to the harming of a great & beautiful potential wilderness area -- perhaps pockets of development -- carefully analyzed as to where ... attempts to make it possible for the Indians to move into the 20th (not the 19th century as the missions seem to be doing) IF and HOW they want to ..... based on anthropological & cultural studies ... It could become a prototype for the rest of the world -- perhaps UN help could be solicited ...

322

My view of man's relation to nature - oct-'70 has to do with nature's processes rather than her form or meaning.. It is to her method of operation not her outward manifestations that we need to relate....

The seesaw relation we have had for milenia with the root source of our being has - after all - been a struggle to explore & disclose this relationship and to try to develop some kind of SCORE To define & systematize it.

We have emerged from nature & we are her children ... thus we maintain a kind of typical LOVE - Hate relationship with her — like a teen-age child we need the security of her warmth #, the stability of her as a source and at another moment we want to be free and on our own and left loose of her disciplines. At times we have counted her at times defied her — mostly taken her for granted as the stable source which would forever nurture us & keep us going.

That seems finally to be not inevitable .. we have begun (I hope deeply enough) to finally realize that this root source is in fact in jeopardy and that by our actions we are permanently destroying her.....

— — - — - —

Honorable Teddy Kollek
Mayor of Jerusalem

on flight from San Francisco
to Washington D.C. Monday Jan 25

Dear Teddy...

Since coming back ~~through~~. I have thought a great deal about our discussions in Jerusalem. ~~I have not had a good opportunity to record for you my impressions of the meetings... this flight I hope will provide me with some quiet time especially if the stewardesses do not (immediately at all events) start plying us with drinks.~~ After leaving you I ~~came back~~ travelled home through North Africa which gave me an opportunity to visit & study some other impressively beautiful walled ancient cities - and particularly Fez & Marrakech which have many similarities to Old Jerusalem. I will speak of these later on But mainly my own interest lie in New Jerusalem. It is here that the future of the city lies -- though the old city has enormous emotional & symbolic importance yet: in area in difficulty, in context, in living importance in complexity the New city poses far more difficult problems than the old. Your own comment to us that we cannot expect you Jerusalemites to ride on donkeys (no matter how charming & picturesque that might be) while the rest of the world forges into the 21st centuries gets at the very core of the issue. It poses the real ~~source~~ horns of the dilemma in my view which have in no way been coped with in the present planning in a visible conceptual way. Thus I believe you are stuck on the horns without knowing why.

Admittedly the presentation was very poor -- it seemed random, not well prepared, shallow, & non-focussed. There probably were many contributory reasons for this all of which excuse the way it was done. Yet most of us have sat through, in our careers, endless presentations both good & bad & you _do_ learn to cut through to the core of what is being presented. I think sub-consciously we all did that here. It left much to be desired.

Unfortunately we too did not give our own critiques in a clear way. We often confused process with product, form with context, organizational set up with objectives. As a result often I found our own intentions unclear & confusing -- as for example the attack on the aesthetic quality of the new housing in Eshkol heights began to sound at one point as ~~though~~ we were being critical of ~~good~~ healthy new housing which of course was not what we meant nor that we want people in Jerusalem to live in slums because they are picturesque. Nor in a profound way were we so much attacking the "arches" phoney as they are Nor the ugly tile. We _did_ all to a man have a great feeling of uneasiness about the relation of the housing to the land, the lack of urbanistic qualities, the insensitivity of it all to the qualities of Jerusalem. I for one felt as if I were looking at all those unpleasantly mediocre developer housing projects I drive through in all the cities I work in throughout the United States.

Well - you may say - why should we be any better than you. And admittedly the struggle of Israel has been to make the Jewish people NORMAL - just like everyone else. So why should your housing be any better than what I see all the time in Brooklyn & Queens? Or your traffic systems have any less traffic jams or your smog be less, your waters less polluted your skyline less ugly, your architecture more sensitive & less egotistical, your environment more sacred your pedestrian systems better, your cities quieter & more humane & less raucous. Why were we so appalled by the horrible things being built in Jerusal I dont know really except for 2 things:

First we all want more for you

than we "want" for ourselves almost
I expect like a parent wants for his
children. Because we feel you deserve it!
and then secondarily of course you asked
us and we could do nothing less than tell
you what we think. We think its terrible!

At the core of everything, I think lies
the fact that you are using the wrong models
for Jerusalem. The model you are using is a
European one founded in the Bauhaus aesthetic —
interlarded a good deal with the urban theories of
Le Corbusier via america .. your architecture, your planning
your traffic planning your urbanism is Non
indigenous. It doesn't fit — neither the landscape nor
the conditions .. I believe also the life style of the
people (altho' for the moment without participatory
involvement processes that is hard to determine)
what is more the model is long gone in
the very areas from which you have taken
them — many of the very places which have
formed the basis for your own work have
been shifting for some time to more
advanced and appropriate forms. You are
copying old fashioned conservative planning & urban
models.... including
the wrong administrative & organizational models —

More & more the indigenous models you have ignored which are under your own noses are being studied and emulated throughout the world — the mediterranean cluster of buildings organized into intricate 3 dimensional architectural villages dense - urban - related to the landscape - inward turning environmentally sound are the patterns I believe that are more appropriate to your own conditions & needs. Within these open spaces for recreation & play, pedestrian precincts secure from the sound & fury of the automobile — view of the landscape from rooves & courtyards can all be developed. It happens that these lend themselves very well to industrial fabrication — see Safdie. The free standing building surrounded by its garden isolated from its neighbor & always accessible at every point to the automobile is in my view the enemy of Jerusalem . . .

Both Meyerovitz & I spoke a great deal about the urban landscape - its relationship to building - the need to integrate the whole complex with transportation . . . I myself cannot separate out these pieces of urban planning though they form discrete pieces yet they must come together into a totality - into a complete symphony if you will where all the instruments are playing together NOT each one by itself . . . the urban landscape I spoke of & believe in is not therefore a matter only of aesthetics though that forms of course a part of it .. It has to do with an entire complex of integrated elements including the aesthetic. Form in my view arrives out of attention to objectives & through a process of working at things — It is not in order to impose an aesthetic form on Jerusalem that I suggest you look at terraced architecture broken into small increments stepping up the hills in 3 dimensional complexes with transportation part of the whole... though I believe it will look better. The point is I believe it will work better — that it will SOLVE more of the basic objectives & parameters that you need to set yourselves... aesthetics, program & function are inextricably linked together —

Chris spoke of setting up principals of action .. I very much agree .. democracy in planning has a great deal to do with that AND participation in running through objectives, scores, & running out alternative futures. It does not as many architects fear imply destroying their own expertise or ability to

design or cope with architectural form or anything else. It _is_ allowing large numbers of people to become involved in determining their environmental futures in a structured way... it overcomes the hang-ups about TASTE & places emphasis on program, ideas, intentions, life style ... it makes decisions VISIBLE before rather than after the fact.....
It involves the people where they can do themselves & the architect-planners the most good. IT makes it possible for them to look at choices not have them decided for them either by TRends or by short-sighted unilateral decision.

In my earlier memo I commented on my fear of trend planning ie: the idea that you note how things are going & then make your plans based on an extrapolation of these trends as if they are facts.. its a sinister way to plan, largely because it gives no options. Your people speak of the automobile as being a sine qua non of progress as if there is no other way.

But that is a kind of self defeating prophecy. If you plan Jerusalem only for the automobile that implies scatteration, suburbanization - every house linked to highways & intricate automobile networks AND then you will be setting up development patterns which will prevent any other system for the foreseeable future... Also its expensive both of land, money, landscape, environment. I suspect thats not what you or the people want for Jerusalem! What I really would have appreciated would have been a discussion based on analysis of alternative futures... with economic, social, philosophical land use + political implications of various courses of action with some universal criteria applied to each so that we could have understood <u>WHAT</u> had been studied <u>HOW</u> it had been studied, <u>WHY</u> conclusions had been reached & upon <u>WHICH</u> data they had been based... there are different terminologies for this way of approaching problems but they all center themselves on a kind of <u>VISIBILITY</u> in decision making:

GAME PLANS + simulation models.
alternative futures
   SCORES
    Etc...
from which you can make thoughtful decisions

based on some clearly enunciated series of
parameters & principals... at which point you
do not feel that what is being decided is
based on some individual's TASTE or opinions
or HANG-UPS — or if they are then at least its
a conscious decision to go with that ! This develops a
city based on community desires & needs & makes architect-planners the vehicle.
I would like to see some operational plan
for the development of Jerusalem including a
clear statement of the cast-of-characters. Who
makes decisions— how are these arrived at — is this
a ~~legally~~ legitimately arrived at way of doing things or simply
the "way things are done".   Who knows about it?
~~Does~~ it involve the community? I sense a
conflict in responsibility between various agencies
of government... how can this be resolved?
In your organizational set up do you have:?

1. A CITY Planning director... with staff— —
2. A planning Commission — A Fine Arts Commission
3. A Zoning board
4. Some body in charge of renewal?
5. Relations between 1/2 & your ~~city~~ council?

HOW is your planning implemented?

Do you have a parking policy?
" " " " citizen participation mechanism?
" " " " authority?

Do
Should you decide to park 400,000 vehicles in
Jerusalem (which your Master Plan says you
should: this WILL occupy

400,000 × 350/sq ft/per car : 3-40,000 Acres /×4
                 3-350   160,000
                                in (usually) 2 places   Dunam
                                origin + destination —

       350
2 0 0 0 0 0 0 0
1 2 0 0 0 0 0
40,000 4 0 0 0 0
      3 0 0 0 0

How do you intend to take care of
this sq. footage — + the highways
necessary to move them about?

With all these things left up in the air &
not even unanswered NOT EVEN RAISED AS ISSUES
how could we in good faith react to the plan?

What is more Jerusalem has as well as
a housing/gov't center/business center role a
regional role as well.... it3 relation to Tel Aviv
is significant... even now the traffic between the
2 cities is significant... No mention of the relationship
                    disturbing
has been mentioned. Britton Harris tried to raise this
       paramount
issue. how do the cities relate— is there a
connecting link? How are the cities related?
Perhaps a linear city with open spaces all

along - like a string of beads -- Jerusalem Ramallah, etc, linked by a rail system (monorail, or other) would be appropriate with nodes as shopping centers ... has this been studied? Has transport integrated into community development been given its due?

The fact is that everyone is uneasy about what is going on. There _is_ no clear administrative framework for planning - I see (or saw) no lines of communication with the citizens No enunciation of objectives, no client, no established commissions, no redevelopment agency no discourses with city council No citizens planning groups..... therefore no real master planning.... because no procedural method in a democracy to carry on meaningful planning. This may ultimately be what _has_ to happen first ... to establish a framework for planning before it can occur in an orderly and significant way.

I think that there were 2 main thrusts that emerged from our group which after all was composed of : { aestheticians a rather mixed group { planners of disciplines { historians { architects

① One thrust emphasized: aesthetics, form quality, character, ambience, symbols & images ... theme became their watchword.

② The other looked hard for: process, organizational set up, objectives, implementation machinery — their watchword was PROCESS
change over time

Neither was satisfied with what happened altho Each had their different ways of saying it
Both are needed !!

I think ② predates ① & needs to be established first.

① without ② can be superficial, inconclusive ephemeral, biased, personalized: styled & short range

But #, must somehow end up with ① as a product
the whole process

Therefore I suggest that you concentrate for a while in the months ahead on phase ② ... establish procedures, set up mechanisms. organization lines of action. necessary commissions, citizens participation
try to list out objectives, purposes, criteria for phase I.
and only when that is done move to the actual planning phase (1)

336

continue letter to
Teddy KOLLEK - flight
from N.Y. back to S.F. - -
Friday Jan. 29th.

I want to come back to my early statement about the Old city.. I think that is a <u>tangential</u> matter & cannot be confused with the main thrust of the problem. The Old city is strong, consistent, picturesque & colorful.. it has, because of the strength of the wall, a kind of organic unity. Also it contains only 20-25,000 people: we all agree its scale must be kept; that cars are to be left outside the walls. Beyond that the issue of stone or not stone of - modern or reminiscent architecture - though important are I insist PERIPHERAL to the really difficult decisions of what happens outside the wall in the NEW CITY. (Incidentally - as an aside - based on my own impressions & then checking these against Fez, Marrakech et al I feel good about keeping a space around the wall BUT urge that this <u>not</u> be a garden or planted with trees - simply a rocky open space in spirit with the indigenous landscape ...)

It is in the new city that the present & the future lies with its difficult problems - given love & affection & care the past will take care of itself

I know of your desire to do the right thing in this the 5th great period of Jerusalems growth. I know that you seek guidance on how to go about it. Given the courage, that you have, you are seeking the way to accomplish what you want to do in this complex issue.

My own feeling is that a planning team should be set up which would have as its task the development of a new Master Plan for Jerusalem. I would suggest that the head of the team be a distinguished planner with Stature & maturity from outside ~~Jerusalem~~ & Israel. With him could be several other specialists equally talented who would work under his leadership.. — ① architect-urbanist ② Transportation planner ③ landscape environmentalist - ecologist ④ Economist - Land-use specialist .... there could be others. This group would work for — I believe 6 months to a year (assuming that the data is available to work from & that much of what has been done is reusable as information)

The planning group would I assume

need to establish an organizational framework to work in including direct lines to & close collaboration with all levels of government AND I would assume the need for the open dialogue necessary for decision making on an integrated basis Consultants for many questions should be brought in as needed.

Objectives & goals development & citizens input as well as official body inputs should start immediately at every level.

Reports on progress + alternative studies should be made visible frequently, during this time. Constant dialogue with the constituents should continue.

This group could well benefit from an impartial advisory Board to whom they would report several times during this period & from whom they could solicit advise, against whom they could test out ideas & from whom they could receive critiques...

I could imagine that this advisory Board could with profit be made up from the Jerusalem Committee.

Of course much depends on the talent & profundity of the

people you select for this task — I will think of proposed names — others can recommend also & will send them on to you under separate cover

Please let me know your reactions & you know my deep affection for you & your (all our) city —

Larry

SCORE FOR A.H's ——⊕→ θ 13' ?.
with Dancers Workshop   Kiddush
                              Fri - Feb 12 - 1971
                        Sunday @ S.R
                        January 31 - 71 .....

SCORE
OBJECTIVE (R) ① relation of sequential order
              of activities . . . .
              ② MAKE VISIBLE the relationship
              between people in space

People {
  CANTOR
  Rabbi
  leaders of congregation
  Performers
  Congregation members . . .
}

Space {
  torah ark platform
  Balcony
  aisles
  Recreation room - secular
  Prayer room - worship
}

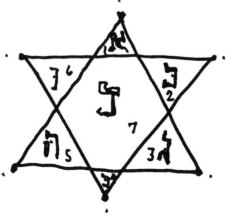

1. Sanctify
2. wash hands
3.

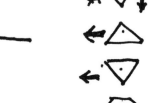

 Sanctify

 wash hands

 Light lights

 Kadish — Extinguish lights

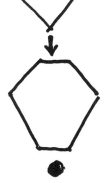

Master score

RSC. HALL

Sanctify - KIDDUSH קידוש

People Symbols :-

K = Cantor
I - individuals in congregation
SH - Sam Brody (Rabbi)
D - Dancers
O● - officers of congregation

~~KIDOSH~~

K I D ~~US~~ H

KÍDOSH   make an acrostic
         or

US- together
K- Cantor
I -
D
H = Harav

SH : Sam Harav
O = officers

Sam Harav

NB
In Hebrew prayers (especially from Medieval times)
traditionally the first letter of each line added
up to a significant symbolic meaning —

SPACE	PARTICIPANTS	ACTIVITIES

1

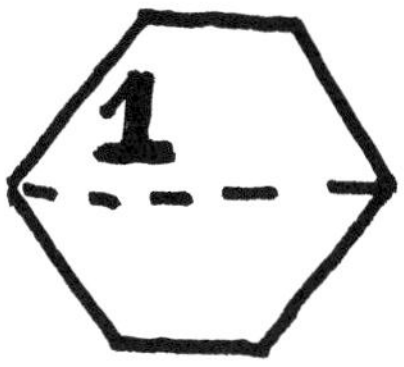

— KIDOSH

SINGING dancing
folk dancing

2

—

K
D + I (10)
O

SH
D + SH + K
others

chants
lead minyan of ten
who join hands
enter worship sp.
"
Washing ritual
anointing

3

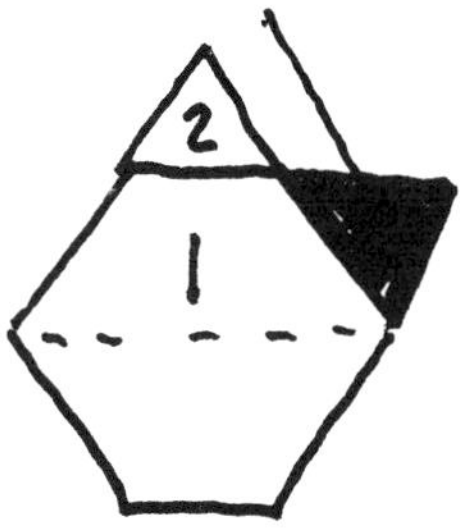

SH
D
D

blessing
light the lights
readings from Torah

4

SH + D

Kaddish

5

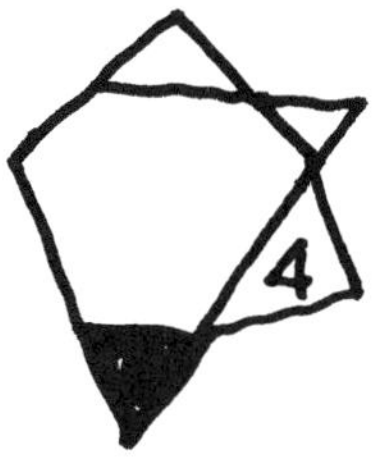

D
D

Relight lights
personal affirmatos

6. ✡ D + SH   Welcome
                      bride
                      Song, dance
                      instruments

         D + O   Bride enters
         + I
         SH

                      chant
                      KADOSH -
7. ✡   D   Adoshem

        SH + I   Shema
        + O

8   ✡   K̸ID OSH   myrtle procession
                      to secular space
                      for food sharing
                      chanting

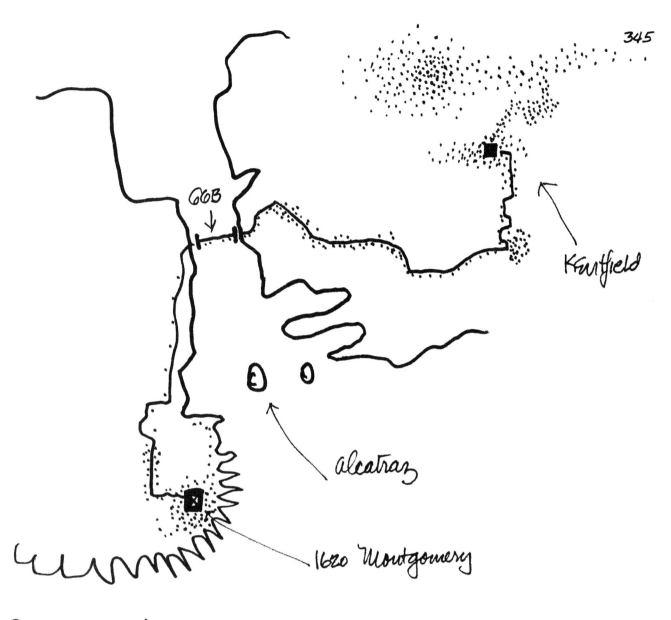

66B

Krutfield

alcatraz

1620 Montgomery

SCORE for day 12 —
Environmental workshop
Leadership training
"Describe your
neighborhood &
perform the description
april 1971

S.F. Bay Area

my neighborhood <u>IS</u> :—

A redwood house in the woods
Looking at mountainalpais
and having it look back at me.
20 years of living —————
The footsteps & laughter of my
    Children . . . . .
The continuity of Ann
The smell of chapparal &
    the spring color of wild lilac
The tall trees at the back of
    the house anchoring the
    Space
The hammock swinging in the
    woods and then the long
    drive to the city ——
    up over the waldo grade
    into the tunnel
The blinding light as you

come out down hill
The excitement of the city seen
   across the bay...Buildings
   Shining white on the hills &
   the golden orange towers
   swirling in the fog....

My neighborhood is the view to
the Farallones looking out to
sea ,

Bay Street from Columbus
and the old Dodd warehouse
nestled under COIT Tower
where I work.......

And my friends all over the
world.

↓

Shown as a movie script...
  with the sounds & smells

My neighborhood is upper middle
class white :— which I don't like ....
anglo saxon predominantly
with a good intermix of
redwood trees

But my friends all over
the world are not...

We live in our houses mostly
or in our gardens .
Smelling the woods &
walking in the forest
watching the deer nibbling on
the geraniums.

We are mostly older or younger
not much in the middle

we have very few community
activities which bind us
together except for our
common love of the out-of-doors

our best time – was when we
joined together in the Tamalpais
creek fight & got busted
together . . . . .

And my Jewishness has no
echo here . . . . neither forward
nor backward

all of that is within me
and inside my house
where my Judaism is —

I WOULD LIKE my neighborhood
TO BE :⟶

interfaces

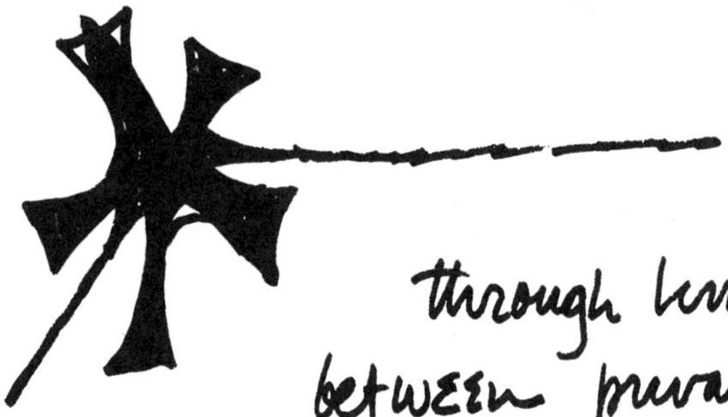

through linkages
between private &
common AND
all
kinds of diversity
of
people -
ages - heritages

MAY 12 - on plane to
wash. D.C..

Alternative
redesigns. un. plaza
fountain

SAN Francisco - Civic Center

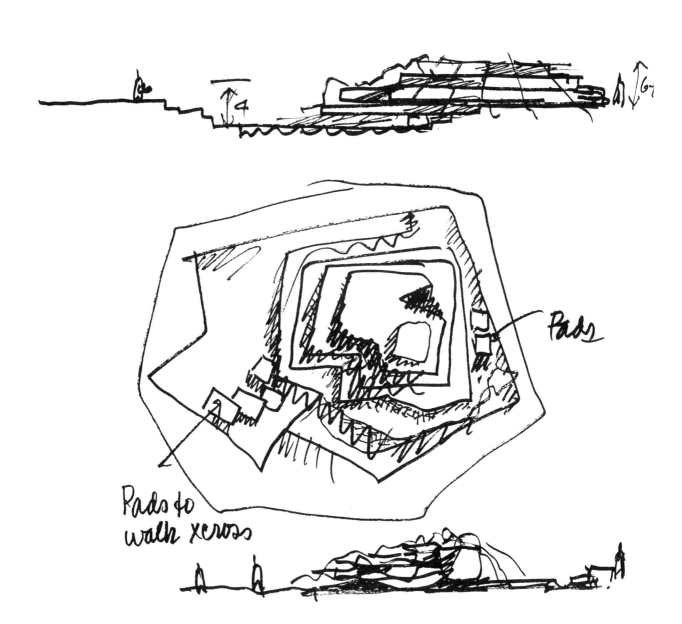

Pads

Pads to
walk xcross

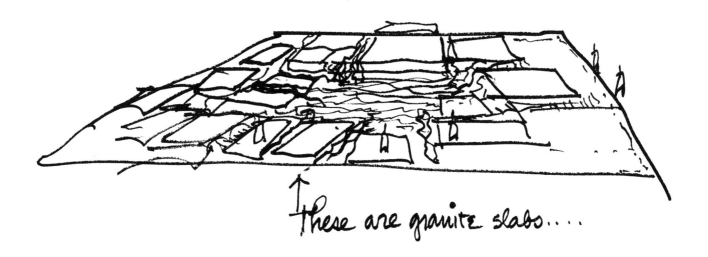

These are granite slabs.....

water at bottoms . . . .

like an extension of the Crown plaza @ Israel museum But 10 x bigger in area . . . . .

Theme is to walk in and around the water courses . variations on a theme diversity in unity — —

or

water flowing.

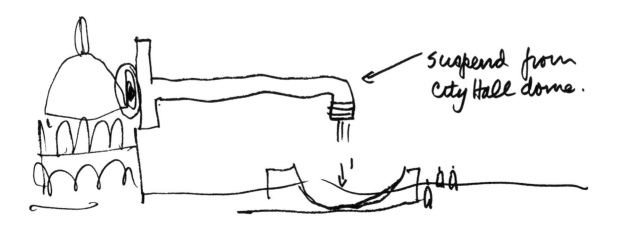

suspend from
city Hall dome.

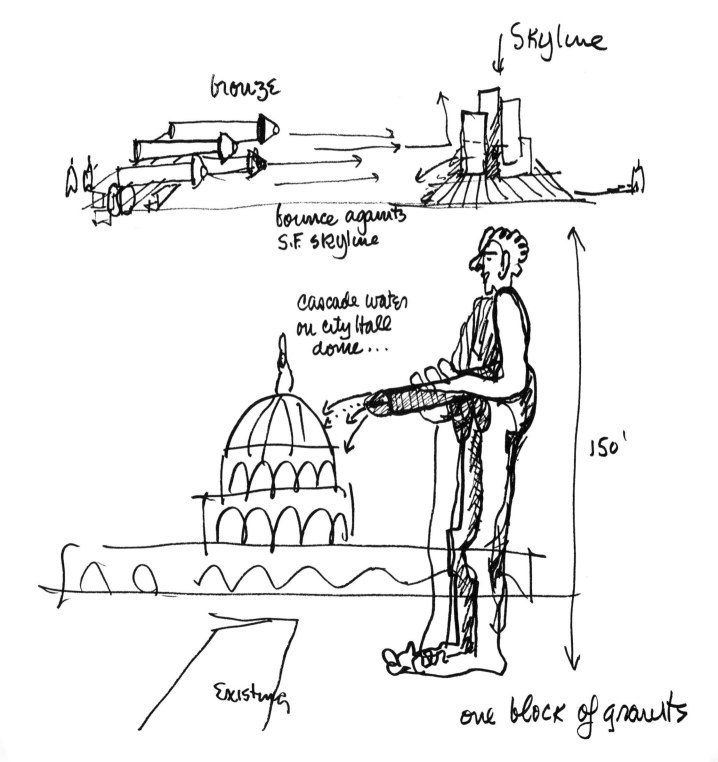

bronze

Skyline

bounce against
S.F. skyline

Cascade water
on city Hall
dome...

150'

Existing

one block of granite

this figure should be
made of gunnitted
concrete - painted
in bright colors...
the face of mosaic
the hair is
water !

3-400
High

water

Introduction

The intent of this evening's event is not so much to TELL you about what we have been doing but TO INVOLVE you in what we DO....

For that reason we have devised a complex score which — through ~~self~~ multiple images, ~~and~~ movies as well as slides, ~~&~~ sounds as well as words — we hope will get you into what we are ~~also~~ into.

The essence of what we do is to evolve form from process. For that reason we lean heavily on the RSVP cycles which is a cyclical &, constantly interacting process of creativity involving change towards objectives. The resulting forces of RSVP evolve from multiple input — they are not goal oriented but process oriented. we do not search for form -- or decisions - or conclusions we let them emerge naturally from how we work.

For that reason much of our work is experimental & takes the form of workshops. These disclose procedures to us & unlock processes. The workshops serve as generators for actual work in the environment

The 2 are linked together — experimental workshops and actual projects .. one relates to the other.

Tonight we will show you examples of both — our experiments AND our finished work --- the both are important to us & the common thread between them is process.

Berkeley
Museum Show

Leadership training workshop

Workshops are ways of learning by doing - not by being lectured at... The essential ingredients of workshopping involves group as well as individual experience... observation of the ways groups interract, form & dissolve, make decisions & involve themselves in process.

The workshop experience is intense and highly emotional.. it makes demands on each person here & now ... it requires trust and the ability to accept the validity of feelings as well as intellect ... it is NOT a head trip. What emerges from workshops ~~are~~ is dependent largely on each participants INPUT.

workshops are active and
involving .. each person in a
workshop is accountable for the
entire group.
workshops are community as well
as individual growth & learning
experience

Here are some leadership training
slides from a 2 week workshop
training experience we all
experienced 2 whs ago ... we
trained ourselves to lead community
workshops in other places so
as to allow ~~something~~ people to
participate in the changing of
their own environments....

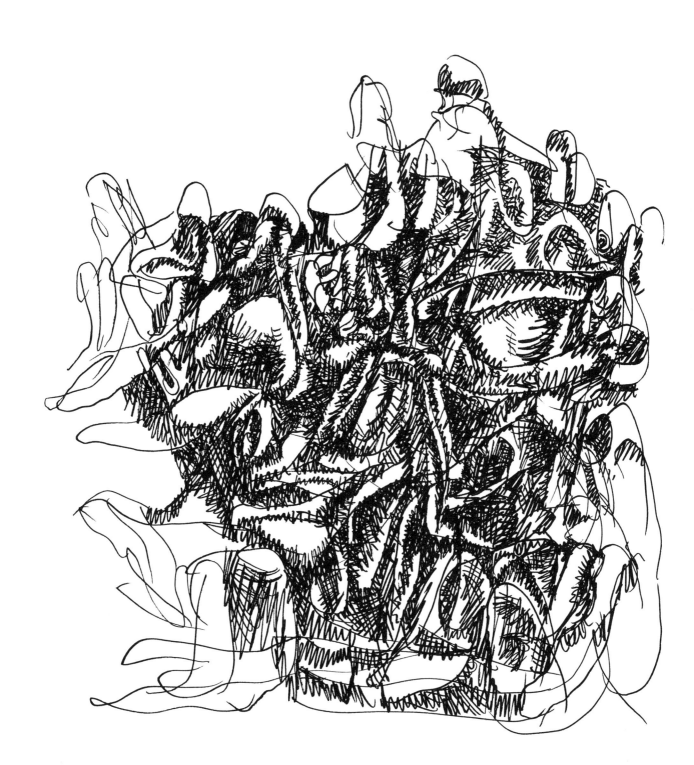

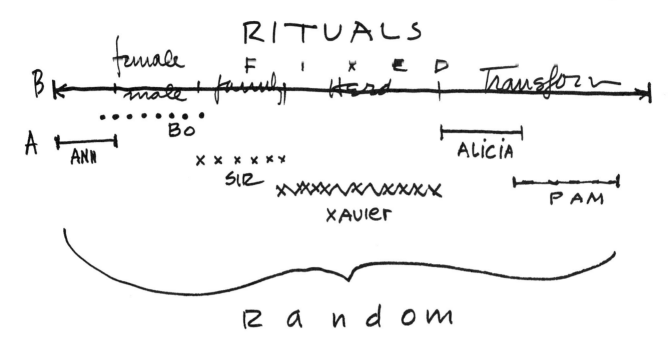

The fixed elements are RITUALS which reflect the stable elements in society the fixed - orderly progressions - both intuitive and organized by society as cultural stables.... the random elements overlain on the fixed ones are occurrences by chance - effortless - non -organized - somewhat chaotic & threatening - non preconceived nor controllable .... LIFE is made up of BOTH.

POINT I - - - LH comments

SOME mention has been made of:

<u>infrastructure</u> .... It is discussed like an alimentary
tract in a person's inside. streets &
1 work in Venezuela - Guayana .. utilities....
2 sometimes roof only - hardest part ...
3 <u>Barrios</u> .. quite interesting - <u>except</u> sewerage
& roads .... no open space as they grow
Now want - (demand is better word)
parks, playgrounds, plazas.

BUT:
Infrastructure does <u>NOT</u> have to be dull --- it is
reflective of the citizens life style -- It
must be more than just a series of conduits
What we have been admiring most is the ancient
greek infrastructure -- the buildings are
gone or decayed....."But the infrastructure
lingers on"

"When our cities lie in ruins will they show
a beautiful infrastructure to future Delos
symposium participants ??"

IN our own modern cities they <u>have</u> been
ignored -- most of us are living off of 19th
century donations ... in the US no major
city park that I know has been done in
the 20th century.. exception - Seattle Center

Now beginning to change - - -

Portland is leading a kind of Renaissance

But they need to function -- as well
as be visually handsome --
activity centers -
sitting areas - plazas - meeting places
NOT Just plazas as foregrounds for
buildings.....
New streets & zones free of cars -- malls
Nicollet --
Roof gardens over underground car parks
the new 3 dimensional net-work
of open spaces in cities ....

POINT II

The relation of structure to the larger
landscape --- <u>SITE</u>

Villages we have seen all have a
close knit relation to the landscape

They really are <u>one</u> building - a mega-
structure made up of parts - same
principle thru'out world - greece
Italy
arab villages
spain . . . .

Plaza   ↖ stairs between
leading down

No cuts - no fills . . .

IN our modern technology we have
destroyed this relationship . . . .

We no longer establish a relationship of
structures to the landscape in any profound
organic or physical or psychological or
behavioral or functional sense . . . this
is > important than question of Hi
versus low - rise . . . . .

At the Delos symposium -
comments to the group

NOTES ON PARTICIPATION ------ LAWRENCE Halprin.

My own interest in participation stems from early experiments in scoring .... scoring meaning the "energizing of processes over time" such as in musical scoring ...... ~~many yrs. ago~~

I first became involved through my need to develop choreographic notations for the new theatre of my wife ... this included not only people motion through space but also - since we were working a great deal in situational theatre where events resulted from actual experience & interaction AT THAT PARTICULAR MOMENT - it became necessary to develop the notion of "open" as against "closed" scoring ... that is - scoring - which includes exterior & constant input by people & events as part of the scoring mechanism --that is - it was not "goal oriented" but "objective" oriented.

This occurred at a time when open scoring was beginning to happen in all the art fields ... in the music of ~~John~~ Cage & others, in the environmental happenings of

Allen Kaprow — in the work of the
concrete poets etc.

What was emerging was an inclusive
rather than an exclusive attitude in art.

This led me directly — of course — to
participatory events in the environment — — —
fountains & plazas & places in which people
were invited into the work on a mult-
sensory not only visual level... it led
on to interest in group dynamics & the interactive possibilities
of group creativity — — the mechanisms of "active
listening" as a way of communication as
opposed to exposition of points of view. It
led away from advocacy into the RSVP
cycles... At each stage "scoring" — — particularly
visible & open scoring was at the core of the process.
we favored change rather than static situations.

Many of these attitudes, I found, had
direct echoes in the approaches of the young
who resist didactic approaches — who treasure
communications & who are vitally searching
for ways of participating in events rather
than intellectualizing about them. Their
form of extrapolation is doing...

In recent years I have been deeply involved in the application of open scoring techniques & involvement & participation in CITY PLANNING. We use the RSVP cycles as a base of operations holding judgment to its proper place in the process -- encouraging input — & scoring: first awareness from which common language arises and then interraction — from which motivations & recycled scores emerge, as ways of developing & observing alternatives with maximum participation. I have worked with groups of various sizes in various cities .... the results have been very rewarding to us & to the people, with whom we have worked.

The work is still experimental on large sustained scales so I cannot yet relate to you how significant on a physical design level it has been in terms of communities: but I CAN assure you that the sense of creative involvement is enormous & releases energy of very hi- levels .. in all kinds of people and at all ages..... it has aroused a great surge of interest in planning & counters the sense of alienation...

End

valley
of Sparta
from
Mishas fort
July · 1971

To KINNERETH valley

Galil - Israel.
SiTing of Crusader
Village - MT. Hermon

note the relationship of this siting to mycenae - ie: surrounded by higher mountains it sits in a kind of saddle about 5-700 ft above the plain looking out to either sea or the valley.

old jewish
quarter ...

Law of Science -- you cannot
apply the knowledge acquired
from one level of complexity
to another level
of complexity ←

"Note -- there is a difference
between similarity & relevance

Alex Reyna

372

Mayor
Teddy Kollek

looking down the Coast
Sea Ranch - Sunday
august 15th ....

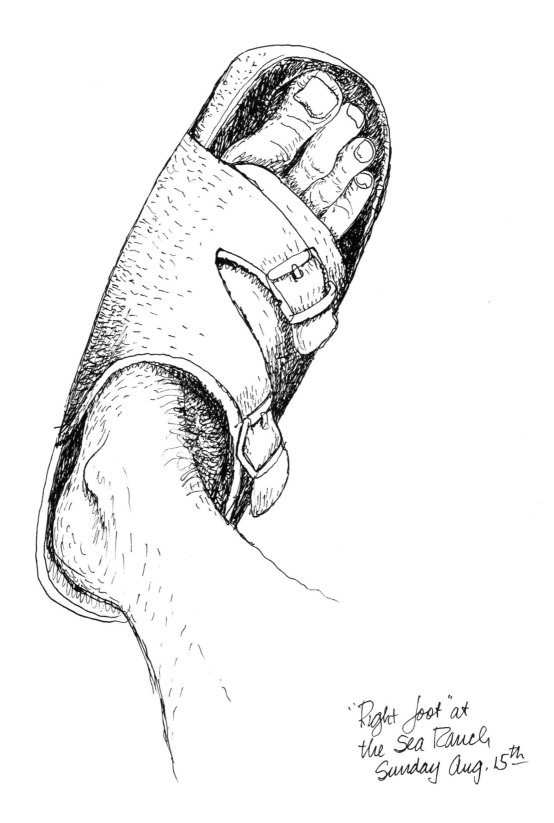

"Right foot" at
the Sea Ranch
Sunday Aug. 15th

Things to do back in the office.

- Write mr. Rojas in Spain -- thanks for invitation to his ranch.
- Call Rose Ets-Hokin re: Louis death . . .
- Xerox Delos 9 --- bind --- send to Doxiadis ←
- Xerox (x) parts of Delos 9 for Jaqueline Tyrrwhit . .
- Xerox (x) parts of Finca Espartero for Doum & Louisa
- Print Carmel Park report -- send 3 copies to Aryeh Dvir.
  (including one copy for Yigael Yadin . . . .) extras for us +
- Send Jerusalem dwgs to Malkah & Alex . . . . . .
- Write Rana, Dana -------
- Finish summary of Carmel report for Yan . . .
  before printing the notes . . .
- Review the Kentfield dialogues with P/c.
- Check out additional material for NOTEBOOK book → Bernz.
- Let Bernz + Ray Bubinow know date my next trip → N.Y.
  to establish meeting time with Planning Comm.
- Call Ed Brenner re: VI payment •• thanks - - -
- Jerry Cohn --- general review ←
- Set up next Bd. Directors meeting.
- Check NCA meeting - let Carlos Campbell know *
  washington dates . .
- Bud Wendell -- let him know when trip → Wilmington
- Sychronize trip with Safdie re: Baltimore . . . . .

Soft rock with
pot holes...
in the cove. S/R
Sun Aug 22.

377

Grandma & Grandpa
at the cliff's edge
Sea Ranch on our
31st anniv. Sept 19

SEA RANCH

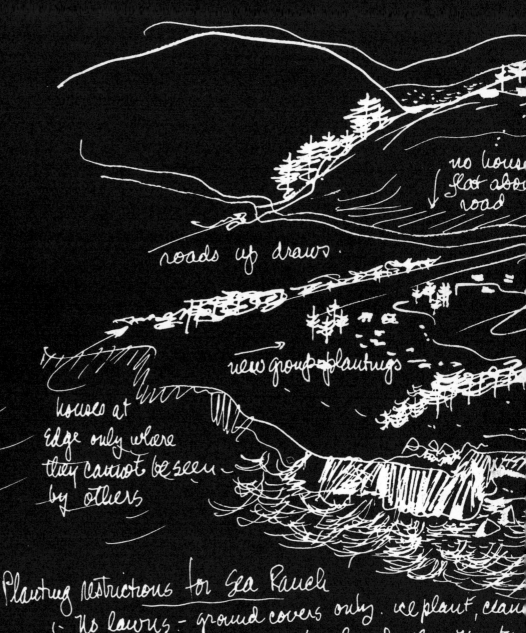

no hous
flat abo
road

roads up draws.

new group plantings

houses at
edge only where
they cannot be seen
by others

Planting restrictions for Sea Ranch
1. No lawns - ground covers only. ice plant, clan
2. Trees only natives or naturalized ie: Montere
3. Shrubs - natives ie: toyon, sweet bay, rhamn